THE CRISIS IN HUMAN AFFAIRS

THE CRISIS IN HUMAN AFFAIRS

By

J. G. BENNETT

HODDER AND STOUGHTON LIMITED
ST. PAUL'S HOUSE, WARWICK SQUARE,
LONDON, E.C.4

νῦν γὰρ δὴ γένος σιδήρεον· οὐδέ ποτ᾽ ἦμαρ
παύσονται καμάτου καὶ ὀϊζύος οὐδέ τι νύκτωρ
φθειρόμενοι . . . . .
καὶ τότε δὴ πρὸς "Ολυμπον ἀπὸ χθονὸς εὐρυοδείης
λευκοῖσιν φαρέεσσι καλυψαμένω χρόα καλόν
ἀθανάτων μετὰ φῦλον ἴτον προλιπόντ᾽ ἀνθρώπους
Αἰδὼς καὶ Νέμεσις.

‘Ησιόδου ῍Εργα καὶ ‘Ημέραι.

First published September 1948
Second impression May 1949

PRINTED AND BOUND IN GREAT BRITAIN FOR HODDER AND STOUGHTON, LIMITED
BY RICHARD CLAY AND COMPANY, LTD., BUNGAY, SUFFOLK.

CONTENTS

v

CONTENTS

PART II

THE COMING OF THE NEW EPOCH

CONTENTS

PROLOGUE

IN August 1919 the Foreign Office withdrew all
consular officers serving on the Intelligence Staff of
the British Army of the Black Sea. This, combined
with a knowledge of Turkish, led to my being placed
in charge of an Intelligence Section working in
Constantinople. Thus began a period of intimate contact both with some of the lesser-known streams of
Islamic life in the Near East and with the remarkable
influx of refugees which poured out of Russia into
Constantinople after the defeat of Denikin's armies. I
had gone to Constantinople intending, as soon as I
should be released from the Army, to return to the
study of mathematics and natural science at Oxford.
The Near East and its opportunities of experience held
me too long. The impact of the new ideas with which
I was brought in touch through my work in Constantinople convinced me that no adequate understanding
of the world in which we live was possible unless a
means could be found to harmonise and build into a
living synthesis the knowledge of the external world
which modern science has to offer and the understanding of inward experience in which the East is
pre-eminent. It appeared to me that this was a task to
which one could devote one's life.

By wonderful good fortune I came in contact in

1921 with a group of students who had arrived from Georgia under the leadership of the most remarkable man I have ever met. Georgy Ivanovitch Gurdjieff. His coming to Constantinople was heralded by the usual gossip of the bazaars. He was said to be a great traveller and a linguist who knew all the Oriental languages, reputed by the Moslems to be a convert to Islam, and by the Christians to be a member of some obscure Nestorian sect. He proved to be neither, and his linguistic attainments stopped short near the Caspian Sea, so that we could converse only with difficulty in a mixture of Azerbaidjan Tartar and Osmanli Turkish. Nevertheless, he unmistakably possessed knowledge very different from that of the itinerant Sheikhs of Persia and Trans-Caspia, whose arrival in Constantinople had been preceded by similar rumours. It was, above all, astonishing to meet a man, almost unacquainted with any Western European language, possessing a working knowledge of physics, chemistry, biology and modern astronomy, and able to make searching comments on the then new and fashionable theory of relativity, and also on the psychology of Sigmund Freud. This struck me all the more as a month or two earlier I had met a famous Sheikh Ali, who had arrived in Constantinople with the reputation of knowing "all the one hundred and twenty sciences", and whom I had discovered to be living in the world of Avicenna and Al Gazzali. He regarded the Copernican model of the solar system as a modern heresy. The contrast in the appearance and plans of the two men was equally striking. Sheikh Ali, who was the very picture of the Eastern sage, with long and copious white beard and a great turban bound in green, was passing through Constantinople to join the Hajj which was then forming for Mecca. Gurdjieff was dark, with shaven head, and heavy eyebrows accentuating the almost hypnotic power of black eyes. His aim was to take his group of students to Paris, London or Berlin.

With Gurdjieff was another remarkable man, P. D. Ouspensky, whose book, *Tertium Organum*, had recently been translated and published in the U.S.A. My active association with their group began when one day Ouspensky came to me with a telegram from Lady Rothermere inviting him to meet her anywhere in the world, but preferably in London—no easy matter in those days for White Russians without a passport. I was able to satisfy our passport authorities that Ouspensky should be accorded special treatment, and he left soon afterwards for London, while Gurdjieff and the majority of their group went to Berlin and, subsequently, to Paris.

I met them all again when I returned to London in 1922, and from then until the outbreak of the war in 1939, I was privileged to study a very remarkable system of ideas which Gurdjieff himself certainly had not invented, but which, as I soon convinced myself, must have had its origin in a school whose sources of knowledge had penetrated deeply into Western thought of the eighteenth and nineteenth centuries, as well as into the traditional knowledge of the East.

When Ouspensky and a number of his students went to America in 1941, I realised that the time had come for me to return to the purpose I had originally formed in 1920 of seeking to reconcile Western science and Eastern knowledge. The study of Gurdjieff's system had made it clear to me that the task was not really one of reconciliation, but of reconstruction, for although both East and West had much that was of value, the foundations of thought throughout the world had crumbled, and it was necessary to dig very deep to find the rock on which to erect a new structure.

The advent of the war, and the signs which were only too evident that it would not resolve but rather accentuate the state of tension in which mankind was living, led me to the conclusion that the knowledge which Gurdjieff had collected should be made available to a wider circle. I had hoped—as I still hope[1]—that, failing Gurdjieff himself, the first publication of Gurdjieff's system would be made by Ouspensky, to whom I owe an incalculable debt for many years of inspired teaching. Passing, and in all cases very inaccurate, references have been made to the system in many books published during the past twenty years. Certainly the public—whether consisting of serious scholars or general readers—is unaware of the remarkable conceptions upon which a comparatively small group of students has been working during the past forty or fifty years.

The lectures which form the subject-matter of the present book were delivered in the autumn of 1946 at

[1] P. D. Ouspensky died 6th November 1947, after this was written.

the inaugural session of the Institute for the Comparative Study of History, Philosophy and the Sciences. This Institute had been formed to continue and extend the work of a group of about one hundred students who, during the war, had been meeting regularly for the study of Gurdjieff's system and of its implications for the period in human history through which we are passing. Though the lectures were based upon the system, they must not be confused with the system itself. The latter, as Gurdjieff was never tired of emphasising, is not a body of doctrine, but a compendium of methods —methods, that is, of bringing about that change in human nature which is implied in what I have called the Psycho-kinetic Principle.

The purpose of this book is to suggest that the time has come when we can no longer ignore the growing estrangement between the visible and the invisible sides of man's nature. The Renaissance confronted Western man with the apparently irreconcilable dualism of mind and matter. In the hands of Galileo and Newton this became the conflict between mechanistic determinism, towards which physical science inevitably tends, and that freedom and responsibility of the individual without which moral philosophy has no meaning. Kant's magnificent failure, in his three Critiques, to resolve the conflict has condemned Western thought to that profound misunderstanding of man's place in the universe which is the root cause of our present crisis. Kant saw, more clearly than his successors, that, until the issue was squarely faced and convincingly resolved, morality and religion must progressively lose their hold on the peoples of the world. The social conflict between rights and obligations is no more than the shadow cast upon our private experience by our failure to make sense of the world in which we live.

A short course of semi-popular lectures could clearly not be the medium for an attempt to resolve these ultimate problems of mankind. My purpose was no more than to show that it is legitimate to feel confident that the problem is not inherently insoluble, but that the solution will require a profound change in our attitude towards man and his nature.

The conclusion that man is little more than a machine, controlled by external influences, asleep, and with virtually no power of choice, will no doubt appear to many as a singularly obnoxious form of pessimism. This is aggravated by the assertion that the very nature of Time is to be the condition of decay and dissolution, thus denying any possible validity to theories of mechanistic evolutionary progress. It is not pessimism to discover that the things we seek in the future are not to be found there, and the pride that we take in human achievements is an illusory and damnable pride. In discarding our illusions we discard nothing that has true value, but, as it has been my main object to show, we open the door to a reality which far surpasses the utmost that mere human hope can dare to conceive.

The key to a positive attitude towards man's destiny is to be found in learning to *take eternity seriously*. To understand eternity means to acquire the conviction that we and the world in which we live have an eternal as well as a temporal life. This conviction belonged in the past mainly to the fortunate participants in true religious experience. These are the fewest of the few. For the majority of mankind eternity is but a word—indeed, a cold word—with little ring of comfort in our present troubles. Nothing but the conviction that eternal life is a reliable refuge accessible to us all if we but choose to seek it can remove once and for ever the bitter taste of life in time.

This conviction will certainly not become general so long as those whose task it is to preach it are but half-hearted in holding it. Nor is it possible to accept the sacrifices which it entails so long as short cuts and easy ways appear to be open. It is in the promise of easy ways to human happiness through what is called "material progress" that the natural and social sciences have betrayed their duty of enlightening mankind. It seems to me, therefore, that it is among scientists first of all that we must seek for a change of attitude. This change should be made easy by the discoveries, in almost every field, which are undermining the megal-anthropic notion that man is the centre of the universe.

In conclusion I must again emphasise that this book is not addressed so much to scholars as to ordinary thinking people who seek to read the signs of the times. I have attempted, not to present a closely reasoned argument, but to suggest a way of thinking which anyone can follow if he feels the need to see the world and his own life in a more positive light than that given by most modern modes of thought.

The lectures themselves were delivered without notes, and I owe a debt of thanks to Miss Rina Hands, who took notes of the lectures and who has succeeded in producing a text which conveys admirably what I said in the lectures—a task which, owing to pressure of other work, I certainly could not have found time to undertake myself.

J. G. BENNETT.

Coombe Springs,
  Kingston-on-Thames.
    August 1947.

Part I
THE ORIGIN OF THE CRISIS

CHAPTER I

THE MEGALANTHROPIC EPOCH

LET us start by considering a self-evident statement. There are some things we know and other things we do not. The things we do not know are of two different kinds : some are too difficult and obscure for us to find, and others too simple and obvious for us to notice. In everything we do and think there are elements so commonplace that we always overlook them. We make mistakes just as frequently through disregarding factors which are too obvious to be noticed as from ignorance. We are now embarking on a discussion of the Crisis in Human Affairs. The crisis itself scarcely needs describing. It has come upon us very largely from causes entering so intimately into our common experience that we overlook them to the point of not even suspecting their existence.

Part I of this book will be devoted to the thesis that we have reached our present serious position through our disregard of certain obvious but unpalatable facts. In Part II I shall explain why I believe that the future course of events will force general recognition of these facts upon mankind. I believe that, although the process may prove very disagreeable and even terrible, the final outcome can be a lasting good if a sufficient number of people recognise the symptoms in time and prepare themselves to meet the situation. Before attempting to develop this thesis I must try to put before you human experience in a new perspective as a background for my approach to the problem.

We can compare human experience to a three-storeyed house. We live on the ground floor, which contains all our stored-up experience, all our knowledge of ourselves and the world, all our language and all the rules by which we think. We penetrate only very seldom to the upper storey, which is the scene of inspiration, or, as it is more soberly called by scientists, "hypothesis formation", the domain of the wholly new. Every man who enters the upper storey becomes a stout Cortes staring with eagle eyes upon new worlds. A very clear description of this experience was given by Sir Laurence Bragg in a broadcast talk a year or two ago. Many of the great creative artists also speak of it, as does Mozart, for instance, in his letters.[1]

The bottom storey, or basement, is another region into which we seldom penetrate. It is the storehouse of all the lumber and, although it is never noticed, it is always there, forming the substratum of all human experience. However clear and definite our thoughts may seem, we cannot think of any one thing without at the same time implying a host of others, which we do not notice, and therefore do not take into account. Every word we speak may be likened to an iceberg; only one-tenth of its meaning is visible above the surface of our thoughts. The rest is submerged in a

[1] Cf. Mozart, *Briefe* (ed. Mohl), pp. 443–4.

20

maze of hidden associations and assumptions, which
are not less important because we take them for
granted. All that happens on the ground floor of the
house, all that we can observe going on in our minds,
will be very untrustworthy if no allowance is made for
its unseen background. The unnoticed implications of
what we say are not necessarily the same for everyone,
and therefore if two people wish to understand one
another, they have to make sure that at least some of the
key words have the same implication for both of them.
Two people may use the same word and think they
mean the same thing by it, but as neither of them will
notice what is in the background, each will soon find,
if they do not take steps to clarify their language, that
what the other says is incomprehensible. We shall,
therefore, have to spend some time in making sure that
we all understand what we mean by a few simple
terms like "man" and "world" and "to be" and "to do".

It is obvious, for example, that the word "man" has
different meanings for people of different training and
outlook. The anthropologist means one thing when he
speaks about "man", and the physiologist means something else. The word has different meanings for the
theologian, who believes in the soul, and for the atheist.
In one context it may quite clearly exclude woman, and
in another it will include all human beings. It may mean
something individual and personal, or it may refer to
man as a species. These differences are quite plain
to see, and it is easy enough to make allowances for
them. The sources of misunderstanding I want you to

21

think about are not these, but the hidden ones that come from assumptions that we do not notice, beginning with certain assumptions we all make when we use the word "man", and which give a definite twist to everything we say and think. I have used the rather uncouth word "megalanthropic" in the title of this chapter, and I include in this all uses of the word "man" which imply that he is supremely important. The megalanthropic view regards man's thoughts, feelings, sufferings and actions as being in some way important to the universe: it is the general view that *man matters*. We shall not yet inquire whether this view is right or wrong, or even partly right and partly wrong; what is important for the moment is to see that, in fact, underlying all we think about man are assumptions about his nature which belong to a particular historical period.

Chart I is based, with a little adaptation in fixing the periods, on the general classification of the civilisations of the past 5,000 years used by Toynbee in his *A Study of History*. These 5,000 years are divided into two equal periods. The first is from about 3000 B.C. to 500 B.C.—that is, one hundred generations— and the second from 500 B.C. to the present day— another hundred generations. The first epoch is commonly called the "ritualistic-sacrificial period", but I have preferred the expression "hemitheandric epoch" to emphasise what—in my view—is its really significant character, namely, that the meaning of human life was conceived in terms of the doings of certain men, demi-gods or heroes and other beings to

	CHINA	INDIA	MIDDLE EAST	EUROPE
Before 1000 B.C.	Honan Oracles Shih Ching	Vedas		
1000 B.C.			Moses (1225 *c.*)	
		Brahmanas (800–400) Kapila (700 *c.*)	Avestas (800 *c.*)	Homer (800 *c.*) Hesiod (700 *c.*)
	Lao Tzŭ			
500 B.C.	Confucius (551–479) Lieh Tzu	Gotama Buddha (563–483)	Deutero Isaiah (550 *c.*)	Pythagoras (500 *c.*) Socrates (469–399)
	Mencius (372–319) Chaung Tzu			
0	Wang Chung (27–97)	Patanjali (150 *c.*)	Jesus Christ	
500 A.D.			Mohammed (573–632)	
	Hui Neng (638–713)			
			El Ashari (873–935)	
1000 A.D.	Chu Hsi (1130–1200)		Jellalledin Rumi (1207–1273)	Maimonides (1135–1204) St. Francis (1181–1226)
1500 A.D.	Wang Yang (1473–1528)	Baba Nanak (1469–1538)		Luther (1483–1541)
			Abd-el-Wahhab (1750 *c.*)	Wesley (1703–1791)

CHART I.—*Origin of the Megalanthropic Epoch.*

23

whom a kind of half-divine status was accorded: the king-priests, hero-kings, divine rulers and so on.

I do not mean by this to suggest that the common man was regarded as mere cannon-fodder whose private welfare could be disregarded, as in some modern doctrines of the State. On the contrary, the great legal codes of the Epoch, such as that of Hammurabi (2084 B.C.), show a careful regard for individual rights and duties. But the code cannot be understood except in terms of the preamble in which Hammurabi describes himself as the friend and colleague of the gods and goddesses of his Empire. The rights and duties of traders and workers, slaves and free, are not inborn natural rights, but rights conferred by the King. They are an expression of the benevolence of the god-man, not of the status of the common man. The central conception of the hemitheandric epoch was thus the complete dependence of the people, both in this life and the next, upon the intervention and protection of the hemitheandros. Even this does not go far enough, for the documents of the period really do not conceive the common man as having any personal destiny at all. In the Egyptian and ancient Chinese inscriptions no mention at all is made of the status of the common people, either in this life or in any religious interpretation of a future existence. The Egyptian Book of the Dead, the early poetry of the Aryan people, the Vedic hymns, the Zendavesta, the Homeric poems, are concerned almost solely with the sacrifices and achievements of heroes

24

and priests. The early Semitic writings of the Old Testament and the records of civilisations from Sumer and Akkad to the fall of Babylon have the same character. The wars of the ancient world were waged between gods, with men as mere instruments of theocratic purposes. In this first period of recorded history the word *man* meant something very different from what it means to us, and was scarcely used at all in the sense in which we use it now.

Then, about the middle of the last millennium before Christ, a strangely powerful surge of new thoughts and new ideas was felt all over the world. During that amazing period, in many ways the most extraordinary in recorded history, a revolution in thought took place all over the world from China to Greece. Chart I shows how the great living religions of the world had their origin 2,500 years, or a hundred generations, ago.[1] To this day more than half the human race lives by the religious and ethical values that were promulgated then, by Lao Tsŭ and Confucius in China, and by Mahavira Jain and Gotama Buddha in India. The writings of the second Isaiah in the Old Testament belong to the same period, which was also the time of the great founders of Greek philosophy, Thales, Anaximander, Pythagoras, Parmenides. All these great men flourished in one century. They may even have known one another. There are traditions that they did, but that we cannot know, although we

[1] Cf. Dean Inge in his critique of Huxley's *The Perennial Philosophy* in *Philosophy* (1947), **22**, 67.

cannot but feel that there is more than fortuitous agreement in the gospels which were preached by this handful of remarkable men.

The underlying unity lies in the teaching that *the individual matters*. Isaiah said (and no such words had been spoken before), "Ho, everyone that thirsteth, come ye to the waters, and he that hath no money, come ye, buy and eat". The last words of the dying Gotama Buddha were, "Work out your own salvation with diligence". All these new teachings introduced the conception that the individual could do something for himself, that he meant something, and they are all characterised by an overwhelming sense of novelty, expressed in Isaiah's words, "Behold I create new heavens and a new earth and the former shall not be remembered nor come into mind". This idea of breaking with an old epoch and ushering in a new was constantly reiterated by all the new prophets from Gotama Buddha to Pythagoras.

The new teachings sowed the seed of the idea that man is important, and not merely a puppet of the gods. The contemptuous references in the Pali Pitakas to gods who came down to be taught, not only by Gotama himself, but by his disciples, shows a complete break with the hemitheandric conceptions of the past.

There was only one country in which this great change of outlook did not appear. Egypt retained its hemitheandric traditions. Persian thought came with the conquest of Cambyses about 529 B.C., but when the conquerors withdrew it returned to its own theocratic rule.

The priests resumed their sway, but the mighty Egyptian civilisation slowly crumbled away until it counted for nothing in the history of the world. It is from other civilisations that the world that we now know has grown.

The great confluence of thought which prepared the way for the foundation of Christianity arose from the new ideas of man which characterise what I have called the Megalanthropic Epoch. In Christian teaching in the West, the doctrine of the importance of man reached its highest pitch of intensity in the doctrine of the common sonship of men to a God who is neither a tribal god nor any of the other gods of the earlier period, but the creator of the whole universe, who, through the blending of Greek and Semitic thought, came also to be regarded as the Father of man. There was no such crystallisation of ideas in the East, where the sense of the independence of individual man developed particularly in the conception of the right of the individual to emancipation. Throughout the East any individual, of whatever class or kind, who decided to withdraw from the world and seek his own highest welfare, was assured, not only of a remarkable degree of freedom from interference or persecution, but also, in most cases, of respect and even veneration. An immense variety of conceptions of the rights and importance of man developed all over the world, but all were based on the same idea and there was nowhere any return to the old hemitheandric superstitions. The "divine" Roman Emperors failed to impress even their own contemporaries.

27

If we made a chart showing the great conquerors of the world, the great founders of dynasties, and compared it with Chart I, we should find nothing coherent; only a jumble of famous names, from which no clear structure could be traced. Chart I gives a structure to the flow of thought and values and human experience, the harvest of which is the world today. Sometimes, it is true, the great conquerors and founders of dynasties produced changes the effects of which lasted for centuries, but more often they swept across the world like a storm, leaving no memorial but a trail of destruction. There is no constructive or coherent pattern in secular history, as distinct from the history of values. This underlines the conclusion that it is by ideas, by the way people think and, above all, by the values they hold, that the course of history is to be interpreted.

Now let us try to trace the growth of these seeds that were sown in the world 2,500 years ago. Let us take in succession dominating human activities of the present day, and see what attitude towards man is implied in each of them.

Science has reached a position of immense power in the last few generations, and has gained its prestige from its practical successes. It is a late-ripening fruit of early Greek thought, and derives from the assumption that it is possible to gain valid and important knowledge by observation, speculation and experiment, *without revelation*. In the pursuit of knowledge the scientist claims to rely entirely on sense experience interpreted and

co-ordinated by hypotheses or theories. Since all knowledge is presumed to arise in human sense experience,
the scientist is led to regard man as the measure of the
universe. This in turn has during the last century
culminated in the view that man is the summit of an
evolutionary sequence. It is true that we find in scientific
work of the best quality a real humility, and a recognition that our present knowledge is nothing compared
with what there is to be known, but everything is nevertheless measured in terms of *man*. It is man's knowledge, man's powers, man—standing on his own
shoulders—who is going to create the new heavens and
the new earth. Notwithstanding all the great differences
in the views of various scientific schools, all have in
common this conception of man as the measure by
which all things are judged.

The study of History is a more ancient discipline,
and it helps us to see the changes which have taken
place in man's attitude to man. In the Homeric poems
and the early books of the Old Testament we find the
history of man as a puppet. Even the limited number of
half-divine men who emerge as individuals are controlled by the will and decisions of gods. In mediaeval
history Providence, the inscrutable purpose of God,
was still seen as the motive power in the historical
process. Gradually historians cut the puppet's strings.
Man began to be regarded as an effective agent,
responsible in relation to the historical process, so
that "good" historical events were conceived as the
benevolent work of good men, and "bad" events the

29

malevolent work of bad men. In this way there developed the doctrine of individual responsibility in relation to the historical process. It began to appear that man could control events, and therefore must be held responsible for them, until finally the historical process came to be understood in terms of human values only, and man was considered important because history is regarded as his history, and because history is, in some way, his own doing. This is a megalanthropic conception of the historical process, for it regards man himself as significant and responsible in determining the course of events.

Now let us turn from general history to that of the social relations of man, the life of communities, the responsibilities of men for one another and themselves, and what are called the Rights of Man. Over the whole of the last 2,500 years we can trace a steady growth of the view that every man has rights, the doctrine of human equality and the importance of every soul. I am not at present concerned with considering whether these beliefs are wrong or right, with or without limitations, but with emphasising their existence and influence. The basis of any present-day consideration of what are called social problems is always the tacit implication or assumption that man matters, that it matters whether people live or die, suffer or are spared suffering. Today even to question this attitude seems strange, but it must be remembered that 3,000 or 4,000 years ago it might have seemed equally strange to ask the question whether or not the joys and sufferings of a man were important except to himself. Here again, then, we find a whole group of human activities, thoughts, and values dominated in the present epoch by the underlying assumption of the importance of man.

In the development of religious doctrines, as well as in secular history, we find this same tendency to attach increasing importance to the life of man, both as an individual and in communities. Religious teachings differ to a great extent from other views we have considered in the emphasis they place on the obligations which go with rights of man, and on the idea that man should be seen as important, not in his own eyes or in terms of his immediate experience, but in the eyes of God or in terms of some eternal valuation beyond this world. Religion teaches that it is certainly presumption, and even the ultimate sin, for man to overrate his own importance, independence and capacity for solving his own problems. Nevertheless, most religious teaching today is fundamentally megalanthropic.[1] The view that man matters to God is the highest conceivable mode of megalanthropism. The doctrine that every soul is infinitely precious is of the same category.

We have no space to discuss every aspect of the megalanthropic tendency, but I hope that I have said enough to show you a line of thought which, if resolutely followed, must lead to the conclusion that, in all our thoughts about man, unnoticed and unspoken, is the

[1] Cf. 2 Thess. ii. 1–12. "The son of perdition who opposeth and exalteth himself above all other" is the true Megalanthropos. St. Paul was free from the megalanthropic delusion.

31

conviction that he is very important. Whether our views
go to the extreme of liberalism and assert the supremacy
of individual rights, or to the opposite extreme of asserting that only in communities, great or small, can there
be rights and the fulfilment of obligations, the basic
conception is the same. Even the most widely conflicting ideologies (as we call them nowadays) agree in
this—that their aim is the welfare of man, and that this
welfare is important. They differ only as to the means
of attaining it.

We can look back now, with one hundred generations behind us, on the period I have called the Megalanthropic Epoch. It has extraordinary achievements to
its credit, but it is in a sorely critical condition today.
If it were not for the general sense of confusion we are
aware of all around us, it might be sufficient to observe
and note the fundamental assumption about man's importance described in this chapter, and then to think
about it no more. But confusion surrounds us and a
crisis does exist, so we are driven to ask questions. If
we wish to attempt to answer them we must be very
clear and careful about the meaning of the terms we
use, so our next step must be to inquire very carefully
into the implications of the megalanthropic view of
man. How far can we regard it as justified in the light
of what we know today about the world, and in the
light of our own experience, and where, if at all, should
we limit or modify it ? In order to answer this question
we must discuss, not so much the general course of
history, as human psychology, the study of man as an

individual. We shall come, I think, to see that the importance of man is real, but that *it lies not in what he is, but in what he can become*. We all have a strong tendency to conceive our values in terms of what we are ; that is the difficulty of megalanthropism, and our failure to distinguish between the values which apply to what we are and the values which apply to what we might be, is the source of much of the present confusion and state of crisis. In the course of the next four or five chapters we shall see whether or not a precise psychological interpretation of megalanthropism can be given in terms of our experience of man and his ways.

CHAPTER II

THE FALLACIES OF MEGALANTHROPISM

WE have to examine the implications of the megal-anthropic attitude to man, without attempting to discuss whether or not it is, in fact, the attitude we generally hold. I cannot hope in the course of twelve short chapters to give detailed proofs of everything I say; all I can do is to give examples or illustrations, and leave it to you either to verify or disprove my statements by your own analysis.

The megalanthropic attitude towards man is based on the view that man is important and valuable to such an extent that "good" means what is good for man, and "bad" what is bad for man. This leads either to the belief that man is supremely important in the universe —which may be called *cosmological megalanthropism*, or that man himself is a wonderful being—which may be called *psychological megalanthropism*.

Cosmological megalanthropism can take two forms. Either we can think about man as the central being of the whole universe, for whom it was created, or we can think about him as the most important inhabitant of the earth. The first was at one time quite widely accepted in the West. It was thought that this planet was the central body of the universe, about which everything else turned, and that man was the most

34

important being on the planet. This was expressed in one way in the *Timaeus* of Plato, and in another in Milton's *Paradise Lost*.

This way of looking at man had some plausibility so long as men thought the earth was the body about which the universe was constructed, but its very basis disappeared with the Copernican revolution in astronomy. It became clear that the earth was not the central massive body of the universe, but just one of a number of planets moving round the sun. Even so, men continued to look on the sun and planets as the all-important astronomical system, and the earth as a peculiarly favoured planet, in spite of the fact that, with the advance of astronomical science, such views became more and more untenable. The hold of megalanthropism on people's minds was so strong that, even as recently as fifty years ago, a great scientist like Wallace could argue that we should look upon the sun as the central body in the Galaxy, and considered it quite plausible that this planet was the only heavenly body on which conditions permitting life were possible.

Today we see that these views are puerile. Popular books by writers like Jeans and Eddington will convince anyone who reads them that our sun is just one undistinguished star among the thousand million suns of the Galaxy, and that the whole of the visible universe, which fills us with wonder when we look out on a starry night, is no more than a drop in the ocean of star systems stretching away to unimaginable distances, beyond anything that we can see. Telescopes and

35

spectroscopes reveal stars, whose light started on its journey to our eyes many million years before man existed on this planet. Knowledge like this reduces to foolishness the notion that our planet, or even our solar system, is of any outstanding importance in the universe. The contention that man is important in relation to all the stars and galaxies involves the outrageous step of denying the inconceivable greatness of the universe discovered by modern astronomy. If we refuse to do this we must cease to justify the projection of human values and conceptions of what is right and what wrong or of what is important and what unimportant to the universe as a whole, and we can no longer return to the naïve megalanthropism of past centuries.

These astronomical immensities chasten our feelings about man, but we can still come back to the surface of the earth, and cling to the thought that he is of importance there. I cannot hope to deal fully with the implications of this assumption, for that would involve us in a detailed study of the time-scales which govern events on the surface of the earth and the time during which man has lived on its surface. It is sufficient for the moment to direct our attention to one particular aspect of our life on the earth—*our relations with the animal world*.

The revolution which came about in human thought 2,500 years ago was characterised by a change in attitude to the individual, but this did not refer only to individual *man*. The various gospels of the middle of the first millennium before Christ were imbued with a

36

feeling of the importance of all things living on the earth. It is perhaps most obvious in Jainism, where the core of the religion is the sanctity of all life and the value of all living beings without distinction. The writer of the *Nirgrantha Pravachana*, one of the sacred books of the Jains, says, "The essence of the conduct of the enlightened is that he does not injure any being. One should only know this much, that non-injury is the whole of religion." Buddhism also taught the equal value of all life. Asoka, the man who was chiefly responsible for making Buddhism a world religion, taught the sanctity of all life and based the whole of his system of government on this. From his Rock Edicts we can reconstruct with unusual vividness a period when no distinction was made between the value of man, of animals and of other living beings on the earth. From the very little that we know of Pythagorean teachings, it seems likely that Pythagoras did not attach any pre-eminence to man, and taught that all living things on the earth should be valued alike. The early texts of Taoism, the Tao Tê Ching, and Chuang Tzŭ and other writings of the fifth to the third century B.C., show a delicate feeling and understanding for everything that lives on the earth, both animal life and plant life.

The sacred literature of all the religions of the period evince a deep realisation that man and the rest of organic life depend intimately on one another, and that their values cannot be understood apart. This realisation has changed with time. In the West the tendency has been to single out man as having great and extra-

37

ordinary value, and to regard animals as being creatures almost below the domain of values. Certain features of the Christian religion have encouraged this attitude, but the trend is noticeable everywhere throughout the period. In recent generations the rights of animals are again beginning to be felt in the West, but even today entirely different attitudes prevail towards the sanctity of human and of animal life. There is a growing tendency to deplore the infliction of suffering on living creatures, but there is very little feeling that animal life is important, or that animals may not be freely killed for food and other requirements of man. There has been no real breakdown of the very sharp distinction between the values which are attributed to human life as opposed to all other forms of life on the earth.

Biological science produces strong evidence for the common origin of man and all other forms of life on the earth, and in ecological studies we find how close is the interlocking and interdependence. As our knowledge of the relationships of organic species advances, it becomes more and more apparent that each thing that lives on the earth requires the presence of every other thing. This applies not only to the animal kingdom, for animals depend on green vegetation for their food, and no species could live long without it. Different species are minutely and delicately adjusted in their interdependence, and it is very difficult to single out man as having any special importance or value. It is much more natural to think of the whole of organic life as one single unit on the surface of the earth, which must

38

be understood as a whole if we are to understand how the earth lives. This idea has often been expressed, but it has been very much disregarded. The German psychologist Gustav Theodor Fechner used it as the basis of the books he wrote towards the end of his life.[1] Anyone who wishes to follow these suggestions further should read *The Biosphere*, written by the Russian geochemist Vernadsky, who shows how we can look upon all life on the earth as a unit, rather than single out man as something peculiar.

It may, of course, be objected that the fact that man is dependent upon the rest of organic life is not evidence against his greater importance. Nevertheless, if the habit we have developed of thinking of man as a being set apart as supremely important could be put out of our minds, and if we were to try to think in purely biological terms of the species that live on the earth and their dependence on one another, I doubt whether we should find any justification for the human prejudice that makes a special selection of man out of all other life on the earth as the sole, or at any rate the main, source of all values.

Cosmological megalanthropism, then, is the view which regards man as all-important in the whole scheme of the universe. It is salutary to reflect that we have no reason for denying that every part of the whole universe may be, on the average, not less interesting and not less important than our earth. If this very plausible hypothesis is true, our knowledge of what is

[1] Cf. *Die Tagesansicht gegenüber der Nachtansicht*, Leipzig, 1879.

39

interesting and significant in the universe may not be more than one ten thousand million millionth part of what there is to be known. This consideration alone should give pause to the cosmological megalanthrope.

Now let us turn to *psychological megalanthropism*. This regards man as a very fine and splendid being because he is more than a thing or an animal, and possesses a permanent conscious self, so that he is not a machine, but a *free* being, with power of choice; and an *effective* being, who can do what he wants and achieve results corresponding to his aims and intentions.

If we could accept these three ideas about man, we should be justified also in accepting psychological megalanthropism ; but before we discuss these three aspects of psychological megalanthropism separately, we must consider in a more general way the possibility of justifying the feeling that man is important because events correspond to his intentions.

We have just emerged from a terrible war, which very few people wanted; on the contrary, its inexorable approach was viewed with horror by the great majority of the world's population ; yet we were powerless to prevent it. This is remarkable because the governments of the most powerful nations in the world were quite certainly peace-loving and anxious, at almost any price, to avoid war. Yet war overtook us, and we must consider whether this gigantic failure of human purposes is to be regarded as a mere accident of history or as an indication that mankind is not able to control its affairs to the extent we like to think it is.

I remember, in connection with the war of 1914–18, discussing this same question with a group of intelligent and enlightened people about twenty-five years ago. Some of us felt that the war was merely the result of mankind's inability to do or control anything or to arrive at any end corresponding to its own intentions and purposes. Others said that this was pessimistic and wrong. They maintained that we should have only to wait a number of years to see the organisation of the League of Nations: this would develop a co-operation between peoples which, at the very least, would certainly prevent war during our lifetimes. But it did not happen so.

When we look back over history, we see how time and time again events which nobody wants, and which those who are apparently most powerful are truly anxious to avoid, continue to overtake the world. If we look at history in this way, we cannot regard recent events as either peculiar or extraordinary, but simply as further confirmation of a process which continues to repeat itself. In everything but human affairs we are ready to adopt and apply the very simple scientific principle that what we see happen over and over again in given circumstances will, in similar circumstances, be very likely to repeat itself. It is on this principle alone that we are confident that the sun will rise tomorrow, that litmus paper will turn red if we dip it in acid, and that from a hen's egg will be hatched a chicken and not a rabbit. How is it, then, that we are not prepared to apply the same principle to human affairs and to accept as a conclusion from the repeated failure of human purposes the fact, or law, that we do not, and never shall, learn from our mistakes?

The reason is obvious. There is nothing particularly uncomfortable about accepting the laws of physics or chemistry or biology, but it would be very uncomfortable to accept as a law of human nature that we can *do nothing*, and that we never have learned, and therefore never will learn, from our mistakes. Such a conclusion would involve us in a change not only in our thoughts, but in our lives, which is a very different matter from accepting the laws of physics or chemistry.

It is possible to say that this wholesale denial of human effectiveness is exaggerated, and that there is, after each failure, a resurgence which reaches to a higher level than that which went before. The waves recede, but they rise higher on the shore next time. We need not discuss whether or not this is true, for it is quite irrelevant to the question of whether or not mankind can do anything. At any given moment of any period what man is concerned with is the immediate civilisation in which he lives, its preservation, its advance, its development, and not the possibility that it will fail and that, a thousand years later, something better will emerge. Therefore, even if there is such a thing as a slow, secular advance, it cannot be connected with human intentions and purposes because our intentions and purposes are much shorter in range and concerned with our immediate lives.

There is also in present-day thought a tendency to

confuse cyclic with secular processes. We tend very often to think that a process which we see moving in a given direction will continue to move indefinitely in that direction, whereas in fact it may be either rising or falling, as a wave rises or falls. The tendency to make mistakes about time-scales and to look at events on too small a scale of time is like someone standing on the seashore watching the tide going out and concluding that the sea is disappearing for ever.

The fact is that, when we look over long periods of history, we see cyclic processes happening over and over again. We can trace the rising of civilisations and empires and religions, their early struggles with difficulties, the acquiring of momentum, the triumphant surge to the maximum activity and success, the onset of inner weakness and corruption, the gradual dissolution and final breakdown and decay. The process is familiar from writings like those of Spengler, but the writers all leave out of account one feature of the process which is very important in considering the problem of whether or not megalanthropic views are justified. They fail to notice the fact that processes do not merely rise and fall, but very often tend, in course of time, *to turn into their own opposites*. This is true particularly of processes which have a clear and well-defined aim, which always move a certain distance towards that aim and then gradually turn away from it. Although they continue to be called by the same name, and people think them to be the same processes, they

43

ultimately become the exact reverse of what they were at first.

These unnoticed reversals of aim have the most serious effect on human affairs, for they tend to occur more frequently in processes where the aim and purpose were originally the best and highest. The Christian Church was founded on the doctrine of the equality of man in common sonship to God and the complete division between Church and State. By the end of the first millennium it had become a great secular power. It had developed a form of jurisprudence inherited from Rome, and with it a thirst for conquest and the ambition of succeeding to the power of the Roman Empire. By the words *in hoc signo*, the Kingdom of God had indeed become the kingdom of this world. By that time very little remained of the original purpose; the Church had not declined or lost its power, but had suffered an actual, though unacknowledged, reversal of aim.

The Crusades were the earliest attempt to rejuvenate Christianity, but the first glorious and romantic Crusade was succeeded by others, in which the original religious purpose was more and more openly abandoned, until finally only the ignorant masses thought that the recovery of the Holy Sepulchre was the objective. The true motive forces became the sack of Constantinople, the opening of trade routes, and the weakening of the Empire. At last, an emperor infected with Moslem ideas and under the ban of excommunication, recovered Jerusalem by a treaty with the unbelievers, while the truly pious king of France appeared as a reactionary fighting in vain for a lost cause. This cycle shows a complete reversal of aim which took place in a relatively short period of time. A general example is the history of dogma, which from St. Paul to Comparative Religion shows how rejected doctrines become commonplaces of orthodox theology. This is equally true of Buddhism and Islam where the heresy of one century becomes the orthodoxy of another.

The tendency for a process to become its own opposite can, without any possible exception, be traced in movements large and small, whether the original aim is well defined or whether it is little more than a desire for betterment and reform. A recent example is the 18th Amendment to the American Constitution. On its introduction it was proclaimed as one of the greatest moral advances made by mankind, yet it resulted not only in a great increase in drunkenness, but also in a terrible wave of crime, which grew until there was almost a threat to the State itself, and the Amendment had to be repealed.

Many more examples can be found in all periods of Eastern history and Western history to show that the more definitely well-intentioned a movement is, the higher the ideals and purposes with which it starts, the more inevitable is its ultimate reversal into a process whose results go completely against the original purpose. This is a terrible conclusion, and one which naturally we should not wish to draw from history, but if it is true we must admit that we are no longer entitled to believe that man, however good his aims and intentions, does what he sets out to do.

Now let us consider the belief that we, in our own individual lives, can do what we want. Let us examine one simple test of the success of human purposes, and consider the promotion of happiness. It is the avowed purpose of all governments to promote happiness, at any rate for their own peoples. It is certainly the intention of each one of us, with very few pathological exceptions, to promote the happiness of our own families and immediate environment. Before we can determine whether we succeed in this aim, or that we succeed better than our ancestors, we must make a distinction between happiness and material welfare. It is nowadays very commonly assumed that to secure people's material welfare is equivalent to securing their highest good. This consideration is the basis of a very great part of our public policy and private endeavours. Now, I myself have been in countries where conditions of life are very hard compared with those we know in this country. In Anatolia, in parts of Greece—not to go farther afield than that—life is very much more difficult than anything people who have not seen it can know; meat is eaten perhaps once or twice a year at the festivals of the Church—or, among the Moslems, at Bairam. There are no facilities for education or recreation as we know it—there is nothing but hard work—and yet I am bound to say that I saw in those places the happiest peoples that I have seen anywhere. I have been to the Easter festivals, to the Bairam festivals;

46

I have seen music and dancing, spontaneous gaiety such as I have never seen anywhere else, and I do not think anyone could be for any length of time among people who live in such conditions and still hold the idea that happiness and material welfare are synonymous. Even in Western Europe it can be the same. There is a village on the bleakest part of the coast of North Norway where, after the Germans had devastated it in the winter of 1944, the people lived in conditions of bitter hardship. They led a most precarious existence, dependent on the chances of fishing, and yet they were full of courage and cheerfulness, and when the Norwegian Government offered to move them to a district where life was easier, they refused to go. On the other hand, I hear from people who visit countries which have the very highest standard of material welfare that they find as much discontent—almost sullenness— as one might expect to find among those living under the harshest conditions. In fact, the happiest people I have seen are those who lived under the most difficult conditions. My own personal experience confirms me in the conclusion that happiness and easy conditions of life are, to say the least of it, not synonymous.

If, then, we leave out of account the factor of material welfare and prosperity, what remains of our present-day life that entitles us to regard it as so greatly superior to the life man led hundreds or even thousands of years ago? It appears to be very doubtful whether, if one were to attempt to strike a balance in terms of happiness, we should be able to give ourselves the

47

credit. If we turn to the individual lives of the people around us, we see again and again how the endeavours of parents to promote the happiness of their children can bring terrible troubles into their lives, and how indifference sometimes leads to happy and successful conditions. If we take happiness as a criterion of success, we are forced to the conclusion that happiness does not correlate at all with human endeavour or intention. Happiness is something quite different: it belongs to a different dimension, if you like.

We must also examine human purposes in relation to the determination of the courses of our lives. If we were the effective beings we tend to think we are, we should expect that the courses of our own lives would correspond to our own decisions. Now the course of our lives can fairly accurately be divided into two kinds of process—one quite mechanical, by which we go on between the walls of habit, where today is determined by yesterday and the seeds of tomorrow are already sown today. There are also what we may call cross-roads, where it looks as if a choice had lain before us, and that it depended on our own decision whether we went this way or that, so that the rest of our life was influenced by the decision.

If these cross-roads do in fact exist, and if our life were really determined by our own choice, we should be justified in thinking we were effective beings. Take, for example, a young man choosing his career. This is to a great extent a cross-road. In the large majority of cases the course he follows is determined by environment or accident, or by impressions he receives in the course of his teaching and from the personal contacts he happens to make at the time when his training or education is coming to an end. Sometimes indeed it does seem to happen differently; there seems really to be a predetermined course, a necessity of following a certain path, even against immense obstacles and difficulties, but if we are sincere when we look back upon our own lives, and when we talk to people who are sincere with us, we always find that there was no real choice. In the one case, we are rudderless ships blown by the wind; in the other, trams travelling along their predestined lines.

In order to understand the problem of choice and the influence of decision, we must learn how to observe our lives honestly. If we do this we see that a time factor or time illusion is involved. We ascribe the exercise of choice to a moment when the choice was already made. The actual decision which commits us to a course of action is usually taken long before we make the overt selection among apparent alternatives. When already committed we often continue to question ourselves and other people about what we should do. This is an imaginary and illusory procedure, but it is very common. In order to see this, it is necessary to make a general study of our own lives, and to try to understand at what time actual commitments were taken. Such a study will always show that the choice was made unconsciously and unintentionally, and that we rationalised it afterwards.

I have not tried to put before you in this chapter a detailed analysis of what I call psychological megal-anthropism. I have preferred only to suggest one or two general lines of thought, because in the next two or three chapters we shall go into our subject more systematically, and discuss the three statements, (1), that man is a self-conscious being, differing from animals, tables and chairs by the possession of a permanent, self-conscious self, (2), that man is a free being with power of choice, and (3), that man is an effective being, able to do and get what he wants.

This may appear to be a very pessimistic view of man. I hope, on the contrary, to convince you that my view is the extreme opposite to pessimism, because it is the view that man is something a great deal more remarkable than a wonderful being. *He is a nothing that can become something.* I shall repeat this point continually so that it is not forgotten. The means by which man can become something are the subject of Part II of this book, but we cannot discuss it adequately so long as we continue to talk on the basis of the view that man already has attributes and powers which in fact he can acquire only as the result of definite and very considerable efforts and sacrifices.

CHAPTER III

THE ILLUSION OF "SELF" IN MAN

SO far I have tried to show you how prone we are to
exaggerate both the importance and the powers of
man. I need hardly point to the significance of this
tendency in our present-day world. We are in a period
of history when more than one important movement,
which began as a positive creative activity, has met with
the fate of losing direction and becoming its own
opposite. It is one of the lessons of history that, when a
process has run down, it cannot be wound up again.
Therefore, if we are to hope for a new positive trend in
human affairs, we must look for the sowing of new
seeds and the ripening of a new harvest.

In order to understand the nature of these seeds we
must turn from the large-scale survey, against the
cosmological and historical background of man, to the
study of man as an individual, the study of psychology.

Whether or not you agree that we cannot control our
affairs, you probably think that the statement itself is
simple and easy to understand. It is by no means
simple, and in trying to understand it we can learn a
great deal both about man and about the triple credo
which constitutes what I call "psychological megalanthropism". This consists in believing, first, that man has
a permanent and conscious self, second, that he is a

51

free being with power of choice, and third, that he is an effective being, able to produce the results that he wants.

We must begin by discussing the meaning of the words "I cannot control". Let us start with the word "I", and try to find out what we mean when we say "I" and thereby assert that we have a self. When we have done that we can go on to consider the words "can" and "cannot", when we shall see that it is not nearly as simple as it looks to give a definite meaning to these words. Lastly, we shall think about words like "control", which imply power over the environment, and over oneself, or power to do things and produce desired results. We must try to see all the implications inherent in such words, and when they can be used with truth and when they imply a falsehood. Before starting these psychological inquiries, however, we must decide the principles upon which all our studies will be based.

The first principle is that we must confine our discussion to facts. Only those things which are given to us in our immediate experience can be regarded as facts. Ideas or theories which we may have either formed for ourselves or heard from other people to explain those facts, are not to be confused with the facts themselves.

The second principle is that each one should seek his facts for himself. I do not want you to accept any assertion of mine as a fact; I want you rather to regard what I say as a pointing of the finger. For example, if

52

I say, "There is a table in front of me", I do not say this to arouse in you any state of belief or acceptance, but to provoke you into a sequence of actions. I want to provoke you to look, to focus your eyes, to go through the process by which you connect your sense impressions with the memories you associate with the word "table"—in other words, I want you to go through the ordinary process of confirming the existence of something to which you are accustomed, and by which you combine all the complicated series of visual impressions into your own awareness of the existence of the table in front of you. Only then can the statement—"Here is a table"—become a *fact* for you.

You will appreciate that to say, "Let us talk only about facts", is not to propose an easy task. On the contrary, the very simplest kind of fact is arrived at only by a very complicated process, and both you and I have to go through the same process, and be reasonably sure that we have gone through the same process, before we can be confident that we are talking about the same facts. It is fairly simple and straightforward when we are talking about things like tables; but we are now going to talk about more difficult things, thoughts, feelings and sensations, and about what is involved in choosing and doing. The facts connected with words of this kind are facts which can be present in the experience of each one of us. They are much more difficult to point to and describe than facts about things like tables, but unless we try to work in this way we shall fall into very great confusion. I shall use

53

words consistent with what I find in my own experience, but if you connect my words with something quite different from your own experience, we shall not understand one another at all.

Adherence to these two principles will involve a great deal of trouble. As far as I am concerned, it will mean saying in rather a complicated way things which may seem very simple. As far as you are concerned, it will mean taking the trouble to verify what I say about such things as are important for the argument, and deciding whether or not you can accept them as facts. You will realise that this amounts to saying that I do not want you to take anything I say on faith. So long as we are discussing psychological questions, everything I say will be of such a character that you can, if you wish to, verify it for yourselves. There may be things which require experience and practice for their verification, and you may not be able to do it at once. When this happens, the second principle should be interpreted in this way. I shall say what I find to be, for myself, a reasonable inference from facts which I have found for myself. It will be for you to decide whether you think my statement is also a reasonable inference from facts which you find for yourselves.

There is one other problem which we have to consider before we can begin our studies, and that is the problem of understanding one another, for it is very difficult to be sure that the words I use will convey the meaning that I intend. Where any word has critical importance, I shall take special pains to try to convey

THE ILLUSION OF "SELF" IN MAN

the meaning I want, but even so there are bound to be gaps between my understanding and that which I succeed in conveying to you. You must allow for this, and recognise that if we want to understand one another a certain amount of effort and work will be required.

With all this in mind, let us now come back to what we mean by the word "I". When I say "I exist", do I mean something more than when I say that a table exists, and if so, how much more? Obviously I have at least as much existence as a table, but have I *more*? I can say I am aware of my own existence, or, at any rate, I am sometimes aware of it. If I could be sure that a table, or a chair, or a stone, was never aware of its own existence, this would give me a criterion. I could say man differs from things because he is sometimes aware of his own existence, while they merely exist without being aware of it. A stone cannot be aware of its existence in the way we are aware of ours, because we know that in being aware of our existence we make use of the complicated apparatus of the nervous system, and a stone has no such mechanism. So we can at least say we are sure that a stone is not aware of its own existence in the same way as we are aware of ours, but that is all. We obviously have no facts, in the sense in which I have defined facts, to tell us whether or not a stone has any inward experience.

We feel confident that other people have an awareness rather like ours, because they have bodies and organs of perception and cognition like ours, and they

55

behave and react to external circumstances as we do. When we are in communication with them they respond to us in the same way as we respond to them, and because they do, we feel confident that they have an awareness similar to our own. This kind of test cannot be applied to any kind of being that has not a body and organs of cognition like ours, which does not behave like us, and we are left with one fact only— that we do not, and we can not, know whether there is any form of awareness in things or beings which are entirely different from ourselves.

We tend, however, to ascribe awareness to things in proportion to their nearness to us. We think the higher animals are more aware than the lower ones, that plants are hardly aware at all, or much less so than animals, and that inanimate objects are not aware at all. We argue throughout by analogy with ourselves, and say that, in so far as we see structure and behaviour at all comparable with our own, we should be ready to admit the presence of awareness, and where we do not see these things we should deny awareness. This is a dubious inferential procedure, and the right thing to say is that we do not know. There is a fable of R. L. Stevenson's in which he describes a being from another planet, who very much annoyed the philosopher who was showing him round the earth by persisting in saying he "liked the people with the green heads best". We cannot help feeling that, although they may not have the awareness we experience, trees have some importance or value for themselves, even if it is a value in which we cannot participate directly through our own awareness.

We must be very cautious in arguing by analogy when we have knowledge only at one single point. We have knowledge of awareness at only the one point of our own inward experience, and in thinking about the awareness of other beings, we make the mistake of trying to draw a line in a definite direction through one single point, disregarding the fact that we can draw as many lines as we like through one point. So we must think about the problem of awareness in some other way, taking the facts of our own experience, without attempting to compare them with what we know must be mere suppositions.

When we look at ourselves and try to find a "self", what we do find is a succession of sensations, thoughts and feelings. If we try to see whether there is something persistent, which stands outside, or behind, these sensations, thoughts and feelings, we cannot put our finger on anything. The more closely we look, the more obvious it becomes that our experience consists simply of a succession of inward processes. David Hume pointed this out very clearly almost exactly 200 years ago in his *Treatise on Human Nature*. In the chapter on "Personal Identity" he emphasises the failure of his own attempts to find anything beyond a succession of processes, and says if anyone else finds it is different he must be a different kind of person. Hume's assertion that we cannot find any self to which to refer our succession of experiences has never been controverted. It is a fact of experience that anyone can verify for himself. Many attempts have been made since Hume's time to interpret his assertion in such a way as to enable the idea of self to be preserved, but if we are to work on the principle of dealing with facts only, we cannot make use of theories which try to explain away the facts. When we try to look for something permanent and persistent alongside the succession of thoughts, feelings and sensations that go on in us, we can see that the body persists, and the name by which we know ourselves continues to be the same, but we cannot find anything inside which persists in the same way.

This reference to body and name may remind some of you that Hume's discovery was anticipated 2,500 years ago by Gotama Buddha, for one of the central teachings of Buddhism is that man has no self. Every school of Buddhism, from Ceylon to China, teaches men to look within themselves and verify that they have no selves, to say of everything that they find, "This is not I, this is no self of mine". They are not taught to do this as an act of faith; they are taught that it is a fact, which each person must prove for himself. It is very remarkable that about a quarter of the world's population—500,000,000 Buddhists and millions of adherents of similar creeds such as Jainism and Zen—should all have been taught for 2,500 years that man has no self, and that no one from among all that great part of the world's population should have risen up to question and disprove it, while we, in the West, have developed so strong a tradition that man has a self, that we talk about ourselves as "I" and "myself" as if we were single permanent beings.

This contrast should at the very least make us look carefully at this question, especially when Western philosophers like Hume, quite independently, and I think without knowing anything of Buddhist teaching, have come to the identical conclusion and recognised that their own experience taught them that they could find no self—no permanent subject watching the stream of experiences.

If this way of approach still does not lead us to any facts about self, we must think about it in another way, for it is very important that we should arrive at the facts.

We can distinguish between "I" and "mine". There are many things about which we say "mine", so if we could in some way draw a circle round ourselves and say, "Everything outside this circle is mine, but inside is I, I myself", we should at last find something which we could talk about as the self. What is simply "mine" is not a self. A table has many things which belong to it—its top, legs, surface, colour, value and so on—but this does not give it a self. I have many things which belong to me, in the same way, and which are important to me, but they do not entitle me to talk about a self. We have not time for a full discussion of the psychology of "I" and "mine", but anyone who is interested, and has not already done so, should read Chapter X of William James's *Principles of Psychology*, in which he considers the problem in great detail, and cites the opinions of many other earlier psychologists.

When we try this experiment of mentally drawing a circle and thinking, "All that is mine is outside the circle and I myself am inside it", it is difficult to find anything to put inside. Our bodies must be outside because we think of them as "mine" and not as "I". We see thoughts going on, weighing things up, good thoughts and bad, and day-dreams, but we do not think about them as "I"; we talk about "my thoughts", "my feelings", so they also are outside the circle. Whenever we find something and say, "This is I", and try to put our finger on it, it becomes "mine", and goes outside the circle, till we are reminded of the last act of *Peer Gynt*, where Peer peels the wild onion and thinks of every skin as one part of him. He goes on, peeling and peeling, and at last he says, "Where is the kernel? I'm blest if it has one: to the innermost centre it is nothing but skins, smaller and smaller". The encounter with the Button Moulder in the same play is very significant, too; to save himself from the Button Moulder, Peer must show that he has a self of his own. Which of us would like to feel confident of doing better than he, of being able to produce a self? Both in the simile of the wild onion, and in any direct attempts we make to find in ourselves something we can call "I" as distinct from "mine", we end with our hands empty. We cannot discover what a self is by this method either.

Let us try beginning at the other end. Let us assume

60

that we really have no self, and then try to discover
why it still seems to us that we have an I, and what it
is that we talk about when we say "I" and "myself".
Here we come up against one of those facts mentioned
in Chapter I, which are so obvious that we fail to see
them. The truth is that we have not one, but many,
selves, and what we call "I" is simply a feeling which
may attach itself anywhere. This "I-feeling" is like a
label, which can be pinned on to any of our psychological states or processes, and whatever it is pinned
to seems important, and says "I", whether it is one of
the noblest and finest states or activities, or one of the
basest and most disavowable. It can be pinned to the
most trivial and fleeting things that have no past and
no future, and then even these say "I". When we come
to understand the sporadic way in which the "I-feeling"
can attach itself anywhere, we shall have found a fact
which shows that the "I-feeling" is no test of a self.

Then we can find another fact, equally easy to verify
and even more important. The "I-feeling" is comparatively rare. We can do all kinds of things without
having any "I-feeling" at all. We can spend hours performing all sorts of complicated actions without any
"I-feeling" being attached to them.

The "I-feeling" is no criterion or proof of a self. It
is purely sporadic in character, and can appear anywhere, without reference to the importance or value of
the place where it appears, and it is comparatively
insignificant in our lives. This may seem a rather
outrageous thing to say, for philosophers tell us that the

"I-feeling" is important; nevertheless we can easily verify its trivial nature by observation.

You can make experiments to see how frequently the "I-feeling" is present in us and how persistent it is. For example, you may have found that when your attention is directed to it, an "I-feeling" very often appears. If you look back from the moment when the "I-feeling" is aroused, you can almost always see how much of an "I-feeling" was present in the immediate past. By making this experiment a sufficient number of times, you will see that when you can catch it in this way our immediate past is almost always without an "I-feeling".

Another experiment is to try to retain the "I-feeling" once it is aroused. You may be doing something—for example, you are reading these lines now—and you can try to retain the "I-feeling" and see how long you feel "I am reading". You will notice that after a few minutes the suggestion recurs to you, but that the "I-feeling" had disappeared in the meantime.

Anyone can make tests and experiments of this kind, and if sufficient trouble is taken they will all lead to the conclusion that, as a fact of experience, the " I-feeling" is comparatively rare. It is also possible to verify the fact that the "I-feeling" is quite indiscriminate in the way in which it attaches itself to our various states. We say, "I think", "I feel", "I do", "I love", "I hate"; each time a different mechanism is brought to bear— sometimes intellectual, sometimes emotional, some- times powerful and sometimes weak—but the "I-feeling" can attach itself to any of them. Once this point is grasped it is obvious that Descartes was entirely wrong when he invoked the "I-feeling" as a proof of our existence as selves. The kind of experiment Descartes made should have led to just the opposite conclusion, but he made the mistake of thinking that because the "I-feeling" is present at a given moment, it either is, or can be, always present. This mistake is easily made, because the "I-feeling" carries with it its own subjective impression and feeling of importance and permanence, and the peculiar characteristic of making whatever it attaches itself to seem important and permanent.

When I say that the "I-feeling" has much less to do with our existence than is usually supposed, I am not, of course, asserting that we do not exist as real and even unique individuals; I simply mean that to know what we really are requires much more accurate observation than the mere realisation that we have this or that feeling about ourselves. These feelings can be very deceptive, and above all they do not refer to any single or permanent "self".

It is also possible to observe that, although we have not one but many selves, we have a number of fairly well defined groupings of experience, formed round strong motives, desires and interests. When these groupings are persistent, and can be observed over fairly long periods in our lives, we may call them "personalities", so, although we have no permanent self, we have a number of fairly stable personalities,

63

which differ from each other both in kind and qualities. We may have personalities constructed round lofty motives—the desire for the best and highest, love of beauty and love of truth ; and others grouped round motives like curiosity—the desire for change and interest in new experiences ; or round motives of quite physical character—such as the desire for activity of the body, or for good food and bodily comfort ; or round such motives as the desire for friendliness. Some people have very clear selves which consist entirely in wanting people to smile at them and like them. When such a personality is active, the only thing that matters is that people should not frown or be unpleasant.

How to study and discriminate between personalities is a practical problem, and we are not concerned with it now. It is sufficient for the moment to try to see how motives and interests are grouped together in us, and how these groupings take the place of the single, permanent self, which we always assume we have. Personalities can be distinguished both by the motives round which they are formed and by other quite definite individual characteristics, which we can learn to recognise in ourselves and in other people. Different personalities have different voices, they use different vocabularies, have different facial expressions and different gestures. They also have different memories. One of the most important lines of evidence against the existence of a single self is the non-integral character of memory. Memory is broken up into a number of separate strata ; each personality can recall its own past quite vividly and remember the events in which it was active, but where its own motives were not at work it can remember only dimly. This is why we often say of events, "It is as if it happened to another person", for such events belong to a personality which is not present at the time of speaking.

Although there is a very great deal more to be said, we cannot go any farther into these distinctions now, but you should by now have sufficient material to be able, if you wish to do so, to set about finding different personalities in yourselves, and recognising how they come and go. Now one is active, now another; one displaces another, and is itself displaced by a third. Different personalities may have quite conflicting and incompatible aims and motives. One begins to do something, and then another appears and undoes it all. A good deal of our lives is spent in this way.

Personalities are the more permanent and stable groups of motives and interests from which we act, but there are many gradations that go down to the most trivial impulses, and if a trivial impulse comes up, and is present without anything else, we have to call this self also. "Selves" therefore can range from being more or less permanent, in the sense that they continue more or less all our lives, through less stable, less persistent forms, down to the most fleeting impulses of like and aversion which may lead us at a given moment to act in a way that is quite unconnected with any permanent motive. The "I-feeling" can attach itself to any one of them which can at that moment take decisions and act on our behalf. Every one of them is entitled to sign a cheque, but all have to meet it.

I shall explain later that, whereas there is nothing that we can call "truly our own" in our personalities, we have also our *essence*, of which we are not conscious, and to which the "I-feeling" is seldom or never attached; it is what we are born with and die with, and is "really and truly ourselves". But it still is not "I".[1]

To try to invoke some permanent "Self of selves" and think of this as "I" is simply a kind of day-dream. It is also very important, but perhaps more difficult than anything else to admit, that not one of these selves is entitled to a higher status than the others, as regards existence. It would be very nice to be able to say, "The personality in me which has the best and highes motives is really I, and the rest are mere intruders", but when we look at the matter squarely, we see there is no difference of existential status which would entitle us to give any one personality pre-eminence over the others. We have to face the fact that the most trivial and undesirable personalities are just as real as those which we are proudest of and think most valuable.

There are various ways in which we can see the consequences of this state of multiplicity in us. One is the relation between decision and action. Where action is deferred, where it does not take place at the time when the decision is made, there is always a possibility

[1] N.B.—The essence is discussed in Chapter IX, where it is shown to be a "pattern of possibilities" and not a present experience of self.

that at that moment of action a different personality or self will be active. When this happens decisions taken by the first self are no longer either effective or operative. The result is that everyone, without exception, decides upon an immensely greater number of actions than they ever actually perform. We frequently decide, for example, how we shall speak in a conversation which we know is going to take place, or how we shall act in circumstances which we know will arise. We decide that some activity we dislike, some habit or stupid way of behaving, must be stopped, or that we must persist in something which we think to be useful. Now, if we observe our behaviour sincerely, we can see that even where no particular difficulty is involved (e.g. the new action does not involve training or some special skill), it happens much more frequently than any of us would willingly recognise, that we do not act in accordance with our decision, but find ourselves doing something quite different. We explain this behaviour in many different ways, but if we will only observe ourselves, we shall see that it is always the same thing—one personality decides, but it may easily fall to another, which has no interest in the original decision, to be present at the moment of action.

One illustration will perhaps make the point clear to you. Suppose I am the kind of person who finds it difficult to get up in the morning; who stays in bed till the last moment, then gets up in a rush and in consequence does things inefficiently. One day this habit produces disagreeable results, and I make up my mind in the evening that tomorrow I will get up an hour earlier. I say to myself, "I know I *can* do it, because if I had a train to catch I would." It is very different when the morning comes. There is an Arabic proverb which says: *Kelam el leyli yamhouh ul nihar*— Dawn wipes out the promise of the dusk. All that I decided the previous night has disappeared. I see no reason at all for getting out of bed at this hour—on the contrary, I feel I should have a very bad headache if I did, and in any case there is no need to get up quite so much earlier than usual. So I just do not do it, because the person who made the decision to get up an hour earlier has gone, and the person who is now there knows nothing about it. Again, in the evening the first person may come back and make the same decision, and again I shall fail to carry it out. Although this may happen time after time, I shall barely even notice the incongruity of it all. Everyone, weak-willed or strong-willed, experiences in his own way this difference between decision and action. Strong-willed people make excuses and say how strong they are to go against their own decision, while the weak consider they have failed, and feel sorry for themselves. Observation will show that these things are not the lot of just one unfortunate kind of human being; they are in the very essence of all human nature.

We find ourselves with one body and one name, but if we are asked what is living in this body, we must answer that we are not one but many—"Our name is legion". Once we grasp the fact of multiplicity, two

68

other things follow: first, we have to modify our attitude towards ourselves and towards man in general. We must not expect so much either from ourselves or from other people, but must make allowances for multiplicity, change and impermanence. Second, we must verify for ourselves whether this state of affairs is inevitable, whether multiplicity is really inherent in human nature, or whether it can be overcome. We shall be able to discuss this last question later, but for the moment it is sufficient to think about the problem of the self. It is perhaps the most important of all the obvious things which we fail to see just because they are obvious, but it is not less important because we fail to see it.

The actual course of our lives and of human affairs is determined by the fact that people have no self, that they are not one, and that the "I-feeling" they sometimes have plays only a minor part in their lives. When we understand this we become more tolerant of ourselves and of other people. We begin to abandon our megalanthropic illusions and to seek for a way of acquiring the inward unity that we lack.

CHAPTER IV

THE POWER OF CHOICE

THE method we followed in our discussion of the meaning of the word "I" may be described as the application of the principle of relativity to psychology, for it recognises that the words we use for expressing psychological facts and processes have a relative and not an absolute meaning. When we talked about the word "self", we saw, as soon as we began to examine it carefully, that there is no absolute meaning in the word, but a whole gamut of possible meanings. We shall find a similar range of meaning for the words "can" and "cannot", which we are to study next.

Let us consider a series of statements in which these words appear, and try to see whether they have a clear meaning which we can all recognise. "A certain piece of steel *can* stand a stress of 30 tons per square inch, but it *cannot* stand a stress of 40 tons per square inch." "A cat *can* climb a tree, but a dog *cannot* climb a tree." "I *can* speak English, but I *cannot* speak Chinese." If we compare these uses of the words "can" and "cannot" we see at once that the meaning changes. In the first statement they merely describe the properties of a certain piece of matter, but as we pass to what a cat *can* do and a dog *cannot*, and to what I *can* do and what I *cannot*, there is a progressive enrichment of meaning.

70

If I now say, "I *can* hold my breath for half a minute, but I *cannot* stop my heart beating for half a minute", the meaning of the words "can" and "cannot" has undergone a further change. The implication of voluntary control has come in, so that in speaking of what I am able and not able to do, we begin to get a little closer to the meaning which attaches to the words "can" and "cannot" when they are used in such phrases as "I can control my life", and "I cannot control my behaviour".

A new, additional implication appears when a habitual smoker says, "I *can* stop smoking", or "I *cannot* stop smoking". When we spoke of stopping breathing, and stopping our hearts beating, the meaning of the statement turned on the distinction between things within and beyond the control of our voluntary muscles, for we know that although we can control our breathing, we can do so only for a certain time, and we cannot control the beating of our hearts at all. When it comes to smoking or not smoking, however, the actual movements involved belong to what we call our voluntary muscles, and the words "can" and "cannot" approximate much more nearly to what we mean when we say we can or cannot control our lives.

These simple statements are sufficient to show that the words "can" and "cannot" must be studied very carefully, and the meaning they are intended to bear must be made very clear in order to ensure that the speaker and the hearer understand one another.

I remember many years ago being with a small

number of people who were studying this question and trying to see to what extent we could or could not do certain kinds of thing. We agreed that those of us who smoked should make the experiment of carrying about with us a case of cigarettes and matches, but trying not to smoke for three or four weeks. When we came to report on the results of the experiment, one man gave an observation which was particularly illuminating for the understanding of the words "can" and "cannot". He said that as he was coming to the discussion that evening, he had sat in the tube train, thinking how very useful the experiment had been ; for it had shown that, contrary to his expectation, if he made up his mind to do so, he could stop smoking, for the desire to smoke soon disappeared. But while he was thinking about reporting his success in the experiment, he happened to look at his hand, and saw he had a lighted cigarette in it! This incident brings out the very important fact that there must be a certain awareness of what we are doing before we can talk about "can" and "cannot" in the sense that is important to us.

The nature of the awareness needed can be verified by a simple experiment. We all of us walk with a pace of a fairly definite length. This has developed into a habitual motor group of actions, and is so stable with most of us that professional surveyors, for example, can measure distances quite accurately by counting their paces. Suppose, then, that we ask ourselves the question, "Can I change the length of my pace?" If we try this experiment, we very soon find that we can do it quite easily so long as we remember what we are trying to do, but if we forget, we revert at once to our ordinary length of pace. This shows us that there is also a factor of memory involved in determining whether I can or cannot carry out the experiment.

One more point must be emphasised before we go any farther. All the things we are talking about now are perfectly possible. We are not asking ourselves whether we can or cannot fly, or whether we can inhale poison gas instead of smoking. We are trying to see how to apply the words "can" and "cannot" to things which are not only possible but easy, such as lengthening one's pace, or doing any of the ordinary things which we do by a series of habitual movements in some different way—such as getting up in the morning and shaving, or washing, or brushing our hair in a different way. It is perfectly easy so long as we remember to do so, but as soon as we forget we revert to the ordinary, habitual way. Let us pin our attention to the use of the words "can" and "cannot" in this particular sense of whether or not we can do things which are within our power, and try to see what conditions are required for doing these things.

Before we can do this, there is one more word which must be defined. I shall use the word "awake" to mean that state in which we are able to choose to do the things which are possible for us. I need to be "awake" to be able to choose to walk with a longer or a shorter pace; for when I forget and return to my habitual way of walking, I am no longer "awake", but "asleep".

We must now decide whether the statement, TO BE AWAKE IS TO BE ABLE TO CHOOSE, is fair and justifiable. It is obvious that when we are asleep in bed we cannot choose, for then dreams come to us, and we are passive spectators of what goes on. When we wake up and begin moving about we still do not in fact choose how we do things. As a rule we do not trouble to apply the test I have suggested. If we did, we should quickly find that a certain collected state of attention is required in order to be able to choose. It is only when this state of attention is present that we can say that we are really awake. Suitably devised experiments show quite clearly that the power of choosing enters at a certain level of attention, and is absent below that level. This important psychological fact was, I think, first noticed among modern philosophers by John Locke,[1] who made it the basis of his discussion about human identity, for he asked in what way we could call a drunken man responsible for his actions if he were not in a state in which he could choose? It is extremely important for our argument that this point should be clearly understood, because much that we shall be discussing later hinges on it.

Instead of thinking about actions and distinctions between "can" and "cannot", let us first follow Locke's example and think about consciousness. Consciousness is clearly associated with choosing and the power of

[1] Cf. John Locke, *An Essay on the Human Understanding*, Book II, Chap. I, 8, 11, 12, 19; Chap. XXVII, 10, 17, 21, 22, 23 (especially II, XXVII, 22).

choice. We do not consider that an unconscious body has the power of choice. We recognise that we cannot impute the power of choice to a living organism if its consciousness is below a certain level, even though it may not be entirely absent.[1] We should not impute the power of choice to a sleep-walker, but we do constantly overlook the self-evident fact that we cannot be conscious unconsciously, or without being aware of it.

If I am to talk about myself as being *conscious*, certain conditions must be fulfilled. First, I must be aware of myself. Second, I must be aware of what I am doing, and of what is going on around me. Third, I must have some degree of independence of time, to give me the power of looking back into the past and seeing how events have led forward to this moment, and also of looking into the future and seeing where events are going. I can call myself conscious only during a period within which these three conditions are fulfilled.

These conditions are also those that permit me to say I have the power of choice; for if I am not aware that I am choosing, actions are at the most no more than the kind of automatic selection we can simulate nowadays by electrical devices like the ticket machines in the Underground. I must be aware that I am choosing before my choice can be called anything more than an automatism. It is not sufficient for me to be inwardly aware of my own thoughts, or even of my actions, and my surroundings, and the way in which

[1] Cf. Locke on the distinction between vegetable, animal and human existence, *op. cit.*

75

my surroundings are acting on me. None of these awarenesses suffices, by itself, to enable me to assert that I am exercising the power of choice. If I cannot connect this given moment both with the memories I have of the past and some insight into the future— not into the distant future but the next minute or half-minute—I cannot be said to choose whether I turn to the right or to the left. This brief examination of consciousness is necessarily incomplete, but it serves to indicate that the conditions for what we may call "self-consciousness" are identical with the conditions of being able to "choose". We are therefore provisionally justified in accepting the definition "to be awake is to be able to choose", even though its full meaning will become apparent only later on.

We can find out by experiment and observation how often and for how long we can be awake. If we select some action which is entirely within our power and where no physical difficulty can prevent us from performing it, we can verify that we can continue to do it for a limited period of time. In order to be quite certain of the accuracy of our observations, we must, of course, choose some action that could not happen of itself, regardless of whether we were choosing to do it or not. A suitable type of experiment is to take a watch and look at the seconds hand, and try both to hold one's attention on the seconds hand and at the same time know that one is looking at it and choosing to look at it. I can easily do that; I can choose to look, know what I am looking at, be aware that I am looking, and know that I intend to go on looking. All the conditions of choice are there, and it is something I do not habitually do. If I try this experiment I find that with a very great effort of attention I can continue, without a break, for about two minutes. If I try to continue longer my attention breaks down entirely, and it is only after an interval, during which my attention has been quite away from the watch or away from myself, that I return to awareness that the watch is there. I thus reach the provisional conclusion that if I try to use my power of choice and say, "I will look at this watch continuously for three minutes", I have undertaken something that I cannot do. In order to convince myself that choice and attention involve one another, I can make further experiments based on the same theme of prolonging the time during which I can carry on an action which will not happen by itself as an automatism. In this way I can eliminate the possibility that my inability to look at the watch for three minutes is due to some peculiarity of watches, or some peculiarity in trying to think, "I am looking at the watch". If you make this experiment yourself, you will begin to understand what I mean by saying to be awake is to be able to choose. You will see that choosing is dependent upon a certain state of attention and is not possible without this state of attention. It will also convince you that you have not the power to stay awake for more than one or two minutes at a time, and that after that you fall back into the state of being not awake, i.e. *asleep*.

It is very important for our understanding of human

77

behaviour that we should realise that the power of choice is limited by our state of wakefulness, and that our state of wakefulness is something very precarious indeed, and not under our control. It may therefore seem strange that these facts are not better known, for they are in no way obscure, and no scientific apparatus is required for their confirmation. They do, however, belong to the category of things that are overlooked simply because they are so obvious that we do not even notice them.

The importance of wakefulness has been and is being taught as one of the central points of many important religious and philosophical systems. It is usually forgotten that the practical psychology of the Gospels is founded on awakening as the starting-point. The injunction γριγορεῖτε δεῦτε in Greek, which in the Authorised Version is rendered as "Watch and pray", really means "Wake up and pray". The crucial importance of learning to be awake is brought out by one of the greatest moments of the Gospel story—the Vigil on the Mount of Olives. Under the greatest possible stress people such as we are are unable to stay awake. We are unable to stay awake and unable to do things which are quite within our power, because our attention goes out of our control. This is also brought home by the terrible prophecy to St. Peter, "Before the cock crow thou shalt deny Me thrice". The incident places a massive emphasis on the need for wakefulness, and on man's inability, even with the best will in the world, to remain awake.

78

Throughout all the practical teachings of the early Christian fathers, as well as throughout the Gospels, and especially in the teachings of the Greek fathers— John Cassian, Hezychius, St. Makarias the Egyptian, St. Anthony the Great, the great Saint Moses—all emphasise the need for the state of wakefulness that is called νῆψις, a term which we translate by the Latin word "sobriety", although the Greek νῆψις really means "wakefulness". There are some very remarkable passages in the Greek fathers which deal with wakefulness as the condition of achieving anything which we set ourselves to do. In the case of monks this refers to prayer and spiritual exercises, but we can say that as far as Christian teaching is concerned, the emphasis on wakefulness could not have been greater, either in the Gospels or in the teachings of the early fathers.

In Buddhism the very word "Buddha" means "awakened". The state of wakefulness, satisampajā, and the need to be mindful and self-possessed in order to choose, form one of the basic precepts of Buddhism. If we were to go through the Sufi and other practical systems of Islam, we should find in them all this same emphasis on wakefulness, as being what distinguishes the responsible man from the man who is not responsible. This is a most striking thing. Another instance is to be found in one of the most beautiful and famous religious poems in the world, the "Katha Upanishad", where a whole stanza is devoted to the praise of the man who is awakened and restrains his senses and controls his thoughts and so reaches his

79

goal, while the man who is unawakened cannot restrain his senses or control his thoughts, and so never reaches the goal. As far as practical religious teaching is concerned, the emphasis on wakefulness has always been there.

The same thing is taught in the great philosophies. It is one of the central features of Spinoza's *Tractate on the Improvement of the Mind*. So anyone who is inclined to think I am laying undue stress on the critical importance of the state of wakefulness and the ability to choose, has only to look at the teachings of religion and philosophy to see that they have always been emphasised as the starting point of any practical attempt to arrive at the control or mastery even of the most ordinary things which have nothing intrinsically difficult in them. It is from these ordinary things that we can best learn the limitation of our power of choice. Everyone thinks he has much more power of choice and a greater degree of free will than he really has. After experimenting, and trying to do things in which the power of choice must be exercised, we must come, and we can do it only slowly, to the conviction that, in fact, we have very little power of choice.

These few examples will enable us to confirm for ourselves, if we will but try, that we are wrong to ascribe to man the property of being a free being, with the power of choice, able to do what he sets out to do. We can verify by experiment that we have no power of choice, and very, very little freedom. As a matter of fact, it would be impossible to explain human life if this were not the case, for events do not turn out at all as one would expect them to do if people were able to choose and carry out their intentions.

This brings us to the third "megalanthropic" notion about man—that he is an effective being, a being able to do what he wants. We must now define what we mean when we say man can or cannot *do*. Up to this point we have discussed only the power of choice at a given moment. We have not discussed any longer-term effective action at all, and it is for such action that the word "doing" is reserved. By *doing* it is quite usual to understand the process of setting before oneself some aim or purpose, and then performing a series of co-ordinated actions for attaining that aim with a reasonable economy of effort. In other words, doing is something more definite and purposeful than mere activity.

I can only say I have *done* something if, *first*, I have set before myself some aim; *second*, I have carried out a series of actions for the attainment of that aim; and *third*, the cost is not incommensurate with the importance of the aim to me.

Let us consider these three conditions more closely. To talk about doing, without an aim, is obviously meaningless. Things may happen to us that we like, or are pleased with, but if we did not set out to do them, we cannot call it *doing*. If we set ourselves an aim but just hope for the best, if we "sail with the wind", and if it happens to be a fair one and takes us to our destination, we cannot call that doing, either. There must be both aim and a series of co-ordinated actions. It may not be so obvious that we cannot call it doing if the expenditure involved in attaining an aim is out of all proportion to the results achieved, but it is quite clear that if I succeed in the aim of throwing away the bath-water only by losing the baby at the same time, I should be rather reluctant to call that successful *doing*.

Now let us see how far, in human activity, we can find *doing* that satisfies these three conditions. It is easy to say at first sight that people really do *do* quite a lot of things, and that all these doubts and scruples are both strange and unnecessary. To see their validity we have to consider the point we have already discussed. We have to consider that if we have no permanent self there cannot be very much meaning in our talk about aims. If I set some aim before myself at this moment, and half an hour later there is a different person here, what will have become of this aim? If between the formulation of an aim and its realisation, years pass and another quite different person is then inhabiting my body, my aim may be realised, but it may no longer be of interest to me, or even, which is much more likely, what I continue to call my aim is not at all the aim which I set myself at the outset.

People very often set themselves some aim such as the attainment of a material purpose. They say, "I want to do this in order that I may do that", "I want to make money in order to be free". Many a man who says this makes money indeed, but is not free. He does not notice it, because he himself has changed. The poor young man who wanted freedom, may have become a rich old man who has forgotten that he ever thought freedom important.

All that we have already said about choosing at a given moment is applicable to the principle of co-ordinated long-term action. If we come to recognise, as we must if we study the problem seriously, that we choose very little, and that by far the greater number of things as far as we are concerned are auto-matisms, we shall see that outside events are, more certainly than it seems in retrospect, just chance crossings of lines. Successful action often turns out to be just a hit-and-miss process.

The fulfilment of aims seldom occurs unless external circumstances are favourable, and, even so, when we come to talk about it we often do so with excessive rationalisation. We call the outcome of a sequence of events, the "aim", if it happens to be pleasant. For example, it is commonly said that Schliemann suc-ceeded over a very long period of time in attaining the objective he had set himself of finding the founda-tions of Troy. If you read his autobiography you will see he did not start with the object of being an archae-ologist at all: he was a linguist. And he did not make his fortune with a view to archaeological research but got it through successful trading during the Crimean War. Later on he was drawn to Troy. He certainly made wonderful discoveries, but to take Schliemann to be an example of a man who set himself a grand aim and afterwards achieved it, is just to take a beautiful fairy story as true. Similar examples can be found in the lives of most famous men. If you study them, you will see time and time again that what is called attainment of aim is in fact a retrospective rationalisation process.

One further point deserves attention, namely the peculiar fact that although we find for ourselves, if we are honest about it, that things seldom turn out as we intended, we still ascribe to other people a success we should not dream of claiming for ourselves. We see things that happen after a period of years in other people's lives and say, "This is a great achievement", although we can see in our own lives that the same sort of thing happens just by a blind concatenation of events.

We are also in a very poor position when it comes to assessing the relation of means to ends. It is fair to say that we usually either get something for nothing, or else we pay a lot and get very little in exchange. In neither case can we call this successful "doing".

The power of doing involves something even more than the power of choice: it involves knowing what to choose. It is much more difficult than anyone imagines to know what to choose in order to produce results. This point can be clearly illustrated from the game of chess. If you watch a weak player, you see that, although after the first dozen or so moves there are widely differing possibilities, he is oblivious of the complexity of the situation. He moves without realising what is involved, and his moves may either be blunders or successful by pure chance. If his opponent is as weak as he is, it is just a matter of waiting to see who makes the greatest blunder first. When you watch a stronger player, the situation is quite different. He knows that, out of the thousands of possible combinations that are available at any moment, only a limited number are important. He knows he must fix his attention on these and think about their tactical consequences and also how they will fit into the strategical plans he has for the game. An inexperienced player will often be quite surprised and unable to understand the moves of the master.

Chess is really a comparatively simple activity, and it has been played by people of astonishing mental powers for several hundred years, and yet, out of the innumerable games that have been played, no game has ever been won except by the mistakes of one of the players.

If this is true about chess, it is not surprising to find that it is also true about life, which is a very much more complicated game. The rules of life are not to be found neatly written down in books which one can buy for sixpence; they are very hard to discover and, strangely enough, no one ever attempts to discover them. We all play as weak players, acting according to our own temperaments: some make attacking moves, some work timidly by defensive moves, and others like to wait and see what will happen; but, however we look at it, life, like chess, cannot be played by any kind of automatic mechanical sequence of actions. Every situation requires not only an examination of the tactical possibilities, but also a feeling for the way things are moving. Some people have this in some directions, other people in others. Some hardly have it at all. When we see the course of events in retrospect we realise that the really effective alternatives are almost always overlooked, so that even where people have had the power of choice, because they are sufficiently awake to try to select, they just have no idea what to choose, and so they often have turned their backs on the very action that might have changed the course of history. I have chosen one or two stories to illustrate this idea. The first is one of the most valuable and instructive stories of the Old Testament—that of Naaman and Elisha:

"So Naaman came with his horses and with his chariot, and stood at the door of the house of Elisha.

"And Elisha sent a messenger unto him, saying, 'Go and wash in Jordan seven times, and thy flesh shall come again to thee, and thou shalt be clean.'

"But Naaman was wroth, and went away, and said, 'Behold, I thought, he will surely come out to me, and stand, and call on the name of the Lord his God, and strike his hand over the place, and recover the leper.

" 'Are not Abana and Pharpar, rivers of Damascus, better than all the waters of Israel? May I not wash in them, and be clean?' So he turned and went away in a rage.

"And his servants came near, and spake unto him, and said, 'My father, if the prophet had bid thee do some great thing, wouldest thou not have done it? how much rather then, when he saith to thee, "Wash, and be clean?"'

"Then went he down, and dipped himself seven times in Jordan, according to the saying of the man of God; and his flesh came again like unto the flesh of a little child, and he was clean."

This illustrates two important characteristics of *doing*; first, that it need not involve anything strange or difficult, and, second, that we can easily fail to perceive what *doing* really involves.

There is also a third point which needs emphasis. Very often, in order to *do*, we are called upon to carry out the very reverse of what we consider to be the appropriate action. This is a very subtle point, and the only good illustration that occurs to me comes from that very remarkable book, *Through the Looking-Glass*, where Alice meets the Red Queen for the first time:

"'I think I'll go and meet her,' said Alice, for, though the flowers were interesting enough, she felt that it would be far grander to have a talk with a real Queen.

"'You ca'n't possibly do that,' said the Rose; '*I* should advise you to walk the other way.'

"This sounded nonsense to Alice, so she said

87

nothing, but set off at once towards the Red Queen. To her surprise, she lost sight of her in a moment, and found herself walking in at the front-door again.

"A little provoked, she drew back, and, after looking everywhere for the Queen (whom she spied out at last, a long way off), she thought she would try the plan, this time, of walking in the opposite direction.

"It succeeded beautifully. She had not been walking a minute before she found herself face to face with the Red Queen, and full in sight of the hill she had been so long aiming at."

Closely connected with this idea is one expressed a little later in the same book, when Alice and the Red Queen have to run as fast as they can to remain in the same place. Both examples have a great depth of meaning beneath their seeming absurdity.

These illustrations bring home to us the fact that although the actions involved in doing, and appropriate for the attainment of aims, are not by any means obvious, yet we all tend to do the obvious thing. The importance of economy of effort for attaining one's aim is shown in Chuang Tzŭ's story about Prince Wen Hui's cook :

"Prince Wen Hui's cook was cutting up a bullock. Every blow of his hand, every heave of his shoulder, every tread of his foot, every thrust of his knee, every sound of the rending flesh, and every note of the movement of the chopper were in perfect harmony—rhythmical like the dance of 'The Mulberry Grove', simultaneous like the chords of the 'Ching Shou'.

" 'Ah, admirable,' said the prince, 'that your art should become so perfect!' The cook laid down his chopper and replied: 'What your servant loves is Tao, which is more advanced than art. When I first began to cut up bullocks, what I saw was simply whole bullocks. After three years' practice, I saw no more bullocks as wholes. At present, I work with my mind, but not with my eyes. The functions of my senses stop; my spirit dominates. Following the natural veins, my chopper slips through the great cavities, slides through the great openings, taking advantage of what is already there. I did not attempt the central veins and their branches, and the connectives between flesh and bone, not to mention the great bones. A good cook changes his chopper once a year, because he cuts. An ordinary cook changes his chopper once a month, because he hacks. Now my chopper has been in use for nineteen years; it has cut up several thousand bullocks; yet its edge is as sharp as if it just came from the whetstone. At the joints there are always interstices, and the edge of the chopper is without thickness. If we insert that which is without thickness into an interstice, there is certainly plenty of room for it to move along. Nevertheless, when I come to a complicated joint, and see that there will be some difficulty, I proceed anxiously and with caution. I fix my eyes on it, I move slowly. Then by a very gentle movement of

89

my chopper, the part is quickly separated, and yields like earth crumbling to the ground. Then standing with the chopper in my hand, I look all round with an air of triumph and satisfaction. Then I wipe my chopper and put it in its sheath.' "

Although these examples may help us to catch a glimpse of the subtleties that are involved in *doing*, the subject remains more difficult to understand than the arguments for and against the existence or non-existence of a self, or the connection between waking and choice. The problem of doing is very strange, not in the sense of being occult or unknowable, but simply because the words which we use, especially in our Indo-European languages, are almost barren of the distinctions needed for talking about doing. We are pitifully lacking in forms of thought which can distinguish between the different kinds of activity required to produce effective results, so we cannot hope to express in ordinary language anything more than a bare indication of this way of looking at things.

When we looked at the historical process, and the affairs of men viewed from the outside, which is the external aspect of doing, we saw the failure and frustration of purposes. When we look inside for the cause or root of this frustration and failure, we find it in psychological megalanthropism. We exaggerate the power and significance of man in three ways—we exaggerate his degree of unity as a being, we exaggerate his consciousness and his power of choice and freedom,

and we exaggerate most of all his effectiveness. He has
done great and extraordinary things, but they are
nothing compared with what happens every day in
Nature, and they are seldom, in any event, connected
with the effective doing of the people who think they
did them.

We shall have to discuss one of the most important
and magnificent activities of man—the scientific
activity, which we respect so much today—and try to
see the connection between human knowledge and
human powers. This will be the subject of the next
chapter. What is knowledge, and what kind of knowledge are we to regard as important, necessary for the
attainment of human welfare?

CHAPTER V

KNOWLEDGE AND BEING

THE last three chapters have been devoted to a discussion of the meaning of the phrase "we cannot control", with the object of bringing into focus three assertions of psychological megalanthropism: first, that man has a permanent, conscious self; second, that he is a free being, able to choose; and, third, that he is an effective being, able to do what he wants. Anyone who chooses can study and verify from his own direct experience whether or not these assertions are true. There are no special difficulties to be overcome, nor have any special techniques to be acquired. No one who observes his own behaviour objectively can fail to see that he is only a succession of selves, and that he has no one *self* which exists more permanently than the others. We can also equally well verify that we are wrong in our customary belief that we and others have, at every given moment, the effective power of choice. By further study we can convince ourselves that the power of choice does exist but requires a certain minimal level of consciousness, which is very seldom present in us. By far the greater part of our life is spent below this level, which I have called "being awake", so that most of the time we are, to all intents and purposes, in a state of sleep; and in saying, the greater part of our lives, I mean by that that the power of choice is effectively present in us for periods that can be counted in seconds a day, rather than in minutes or hours.

The third aspect of psychological megalanthropism is the belief that man can *do*, that he is effectively able to set aims before himself and achieve those aims with economy of effort, or without sacrificing other things which matter at least as much as the result accomplished.

In the game of chess, we have already seen how there is a very great difference between the master player, who knows what he is doing, and the ordinary player, who is relatively blind to the consequences of his moves. In life we are all bad players, for we do not even know the rules of the game, the laws that determine the effectiveness of human activity. We do not know what life requires us to do, or why; nor do we know how to act, or when. We do not even know what the game is or, indeed, whether there is a game at all.

This brings us face to face with the next fundamental question, What do we mean by *knowledge*? We must recognise that the word "knowledge" has no single absolute meaning; it is relative; so we must first agree on which we intend out of the various senses in which the word is used. By "knowledge" we may merely mean the putting in order of any data of the experience derived from our sense perceptions; but we can also talk about knowledge as the basis for effective action. I propose to distinguish between these two kinds of knowledge, calling passive knowledge by the name of "information", and reserving the word

93

"knowledge" for situations in which action is determined by what we know. *Information* can be of diverse kinds. It can be simple and immediate, like the sense perception that there is a patch of colour in front of me. It can go beyond that, and I can be "aware" that this patch of colour is, say, a table. There are innumerable other kinds of passive experience of this sort. For instance, I can know that coffee is grown in Brazil, Arabia and India. This is information; but if I learn to recognise the shape, smell and taste of coffee-beans from Mocha and Mysore, and know how to blend coffee to give a certain flavour, I should call that "knowledge", because it is a formative influence which enters into my own activity.

From reading books I can learn that Socrates died in 399 B.C. and that he lived and taught in Athens for many years before that date. Now let us compare this information with the kind of situation that might arise from an intimate study of the Socratic *Dialogues of Plato* and *Xenophon* and other contemporary Greek literature. Trying to enter into the life of Athens of that time and finding the way in which Socrates looked at the world and in which he tried to understand things —the methods which he used for teaching himself and other people—can induce a certain attitude of mind, a way of thinking of my own, and I might find myself adopting something of the attitude towards life by which Socrates himself lived. When the results of my study began to enter into my own activity I could say that I "know" something about Socrates.

94

This example illustrates the further point that "knowledge" does not necessarily appear in an outward activity, like making coffee, but may be an inward process, a way of thinking, an attitude to the world. The distinction between information and knowledge cannot be defined in terms of external activity, but is characterised by the passive nature of information and the active nature of knowledge. Information at its best is only "knowing what"; knowledge, as I have defined it, is also "knowing how".

We must now inquire whether there are not different kinds, or rather different degrees, in "knowing how". We can distinguish between things which everyone knows how to do, such as eating their dinner, and things no one knows how to do, such as preventing war. Even in the special sense of "knowing how" we must still recognise a relativity of knowledge. There are different grades, levels or orders of the knowledge which determines the effectiveness of our activity.

The first level of knowledge may be called "vegetative knowledge". This we share with every other kind of living organism. Its crudest form is seen in what are called tropisms in biology—the knowledge of the root that grows downwards, of the animal that holds itself in a certain direction in relation to the earth, and of the simple nutritional and reproductive processes shared by all living organisms alike. It is a form of active knowledge because it determines the behaviour of living organisms, and is absent in inanimate things.

The second stage is "animal knowledge". This is the

knowledge that is acquired by what Pavlov calls "the conditioning of reflexes", and, generally speaking, it is possible only for animals with a nervous system. It is therefore a form of knowledge that we share with all other vertebrate animals. It turns out that a large number of processes that we are inclined to regard as being characteristically human are, when we come to study them, found to be shared with all the other vertebrates. Animal knowledge is distinguished from vegetative knowledge by the fact that it must be learned, in the way that a child learns to walk and to use all the other processes that are developed through imitation, repetition and adaptation.

Next we have "pragmatic knowledge", which is characteristically human. It is by this knowledge that we live on the ordinary human level, for it includes knowledge of language as a means of communication and the use of the mind in thinking. All the special skills we acquire for the exercise of our vocations or professions are characteristic of human beings, for they are dependent upon the complexity of the cerebral hemispheres, which distinguishes the brain of man from that of the rest of the animal world, enabling him to learn an infinitely greater number of things.

Pragmatic knowledge is quite distinct from the fourth kind, which may be called axiological knowledge or "knowledge of values"—that is, knowledge of what is important and what is not important. This fourth kind of knowledge is not obtained in the same way as the third, and there is nothing in the mechanism

96

of our central nervous system which determines that we should have knowledge of this kind. Although pragmatic knowledge gives us the means by which we adapt ourselves to life in human society and enjoy ordinary normal life, it does not by itself alone involve any exercise of the power of choice. Obviously if we intend, at a given moment, to make a choice, our problem is to distinguish between what is of greater or lesser importance. For this, knowledge of values is necessary, but even this is not sufficient to produce desired results. It can often happen that we have knowledge of values and know what is to be desired in a given situation, but do not know how to attain this end.

A very vital distinction, which I will discuss later, is involved here. There is thus a fifth kind of knowledge, the knowledge by which effectual work becomes possible, work which goes beyond the ordinary mechanical processes of our everyday life. The fifth kind of knowledge may be called "effectual knowledge".

The significance of effectual knowledge entirely escapes our ordinary thinking. The most subtle and perhaps the most ineradicable of our megalanthropic illusions is the belief that we can "do". This is why it may appear strange to some of you that I should place effectual knowledge so high in the scale and divide it from pragmatic knowledge by the intermediate stage of value knowledge. In the preceding chapter I tried to show you that effectual knowledge is quite absent from our ordinary experience. Pragmatic knowledge is sufficient to enable us to make weapons, effectual knowledge would be needed to prevent wars. The desire for the welfare of other people comes from value knowledge, the ability to give them real help requires effectual knowledge. St. Paul said, "For that which I do, I allow not; for what I would, that do I not; but what I hate, that I do. . . . O wretched man that I am!" In these words is the deep recognition of that absence of effectual knowledge in our inner life, which is no less certain than our inability to act effectually in outward things.

These distinctions have a profound significance for us at the present time. Throughout the world there is recognition that all is not well with the state of mankind. More books on this subject are being written than ever before. The writers emphasise in different degree the importance of pragmatic knowledge and the need for a deeper sense of values. Many of the books show a penetrating insight into the failure of human purposes and the impossibility of achieving a common understanding in the absence of common values. But they all—without a single exception—fall short abruptly when they come to the question of effective action. Most authors propose some kind of solution—political action, religious revival, centralisation or decentralisation, advance or withdrawal—but every solution fails dismally to pass the test of "effectual knowledge". "The wounded surgeon plies the steel that questions the distempered part", but his hand has no power either to cut or to abstain from cutting. The most urgent lesson that we must learn and

98

never forget is that "doing" is something far more difficult and remote than pragmatic knowledge, or even knowledge of values.

Although the three kinds of knowledge—pragmatic, axiological and effectual—are so different in their nature, they have this in common: they are all accessible to our understanding. We are quite capable of picturing what life would be if our values were clear and certain and if we knew how to act effectively on the basis of those values, but to understand our true position we must realise that our values are confused and unstable, and that we are all ineffectual in our private and our public lives. This is the difficult part of the lesson.

Once this lesson has been learned we can pass on to the consideration of a sixth possibility. I have called this "transcendental knowledge" because its very nature is to go beyond ordinary human experience. A few examples will show how this idea can be approached.

We can know from direct observation what is going on in our own minds. But to form any idea of what is going on in other people's minds we have to rely on some physical reaction on their part—the words they speak, their gestures, their facial movements or the expression of their eyes. In the process of cognition we have to rely on a certain chain of events. First, it is necessary that what is going on in their minds should lead to physical movement; second, we must perceive this physical movement with our own senses; third,

99

we have to interpret it as a sign, and in doing so we can use only the analogy of our own experience. This means that if somebody makes a certain kind of grimace, it indicates that he is having the same kind of toothache as I have when I make such a grimace, and that the sequence of words he uses means that he is thinking the same thoughts as I should express by these words. The only access we normally have to other minds comes about in that way.[1] All three links in the chain are obviously fallible.

It can easily happen that people do not react externally in a way that corresponds to what is going on in their minds, and it is quite likely that our senses will fail to perceive exactly the movements they make. I may listen to what people say, but fail to hear their tone of voice, and so miss what they wish to convey. The third link is probably the most uncertain of all. It is very dangerous to assume that reliable conclusions can be drawn as to what is going on in other people's minds by analogy from our own experience and behaviour, for we know quite well that even when we are with people with whom we are intimately acquainted and in the closest sympathy, things can be going on in our minds that they do not even suspect; the converse must also be true. So, although we have only a precarious, indirect knowledge of what is going on in other people's minds, we have no reason to

[1] Compare in this connection the fascinating discussion of "Other Minds" by John Wisdom in *Mind*, 1941, Vol. L, and other articles on "Therapeutic Positivism".

doubt that something does go on. To have direct access to this would require a process which we do not know, and which, if it were possible, would revolutionise human life and make most human relationships, as we now know them, completely impossible. This simple example shows that we can describe a form of knowledge which would require a mechanism that we do not possess.

Let us take another example: knowledge of the future. We all have knowledge of what is called the "specious present"—that is, a short period of time around the present moment. We have direct knowledge through our thoughts and senses of what is going on in the world and, by looking inwards, of what is going on in our own minds. We can know something of the past from memory, but of the future our knowledge can be only very precarious and unsatisfactory. When we examine our past expectations closely it is remarkable how almost invariably they have been falsified by the actual events. Experts are seldom able to predict the future course of events—except when very large numbers are concerned and only statistical relationships involved. We can say that the future is predictable only when it is uninteresting.

It may be argued that we cannot know the future because the future does not exist, but such a view has become almost untenable in a scientific sense. The principle of relativity greatly, though not entirely, weakens the notion of the absolute future; what is more important is that the establishment of the physical laws of conservation have shown that the past, present and future are linked in such a way that it is impossible to speak of the future as non-existent without speaking of the past and present as non-existent also. Scientifically we can no longer think about the future simply as a void in which events that have not yet taken place will occur. We must admit that the future exists, although we do not know it.

We know, least of all, our own future behaviour and that of the people with whom we are most closely concerned. We may be able to calculate the exact place and time when there will be an eclipse of the sun hundreds of years hence, but we cannot calculate with any certainty at all what we shall be thinking at this moment tomorrow night, or what decisions and actions we shall take even in circumstances which we can see are likely to arise. If we could know the future in regard to the things which affect our own lives and the lives of people with whom we are closely concerned, there would clearly be a transformation in human affairs even more revolutionary than that which would take place if we knew what was going on in other people's minds. If knowledge of the future were possible—and I am not saying that it is—it would belong to the category of what I have called transcendental knowledge.

Let us take one more example. At all times in human history, man has been concerned with the ultimate destiny of the individual—whether or not, and, if so, how, he can be said to exist after or beyond the end of physical life on the earth. This is possibly even more important than the other two kinds of transcendental knowledge. If we knew that our experience was to continue in a particular manner beyond this life it would have a decisive effect upon our actions, and if we knew that it would cease altogether, it would also have a decisive effect. But we do not know. We stand in substantially the same position as Socrates, discussing this very question 2,400 years ago. We can produce reasons for coming to this or that conclusion, but if we question our premises, we can see that we are making the same kind of precarious calculations as we did in the case of other minds, and of the future, and that these calculations must be founded on an even more precarious basis and depend on an even more uncertain chain of relationships. I am, of course, speaking of knowledge and not the emotional attitude that is called "faith".

Nevertheless, though transcendental knowledge goes beyond anything that we ordinarily know in human experience, it is not so inaccessible that we cannot think about it. We do not find it impossible to think about other minds, the future and knowledge of life beyond this.

Even these six kinds of knowledge do not exhaust all possible categories. "Ultimate" knowledge still remains. Knowledge of this order would be required to answer such a question as, "Why does the Universe exist?" We now have before us seven orders of knowledge:

I. VEGETATIVE KNOWLEDGE

II. ANIMAL KNOWLEDGE

III. PRAGMATIC KNOWLEDGE
IV. KNOWLEDGE OF VALUES
V. EFFECTUAL KNOWLEDGE
VI. TRANSCENDENTAL KNOWLEDGE
VII. ULTIMATE KNOWLEDGE

Let us see now what bearing all this has upon what we call "scientific knowledge" in the domain of natural science or sociological and historical inquiry. When we talk about the scientific view, or scientific activity, we are talking about the acquisition and use of knowledge of a certain kind—knowledge, that is, distinct from "information" or a passive "knowing what". Scientific activity is concerned with "knowing how", or active knowledge. Clearly it is not concerned with all seven steps in the scale of knowledge we have considered. In point of fact, it is concerned only with the third kind, that is, pragmatic knowledge. It does not, for example, include any knowledge of values, for it is an axiom of scientific methodology, in natural science in particular, that personal views or beliefs should not be allowed to influence the investigator. For the natural scientist the word "ought" does not exist; the whole of his activity is concerned with knowledge as such without consideration of its value. His methods essentially confine him to extending knowledge gained through the senses and derived from the working of the cerebral hemispheres. However much the data he may have for his work may be extended by the use of various instruments and apparatus, they all depend

104

on his sense perceptions and are all of the one character.

Now let us turn to social science. Here some confusion may exist between the establishment of social data as part of scientific activity and the study of the social problem of what people should and actually do live for. A great deal of difficulty, both in the methodology and in the application of the results of social science, arises from a failure to distinguish between the pragmatic aspect—that is, the acquisition of knowledge of the working of human affairs in individuals and in communities—and the "value" aspect, which is concerned with the assessment of what is important and what is not important in itself.

So far as methodology is concerned, social science differs from natural science only in that it uses one additional source of information—knowledge from private experience. In addition to sense observation and inference, we make use in social science of analogy from our own experience. The dangers and uncertainties which attend any attempt to interpret other people's behaviour and actions by analogy with our own experience have already been pointed out. Obviously, then, if we are concerned with the problem of promoting the contentment, well-being and happiness of other people, we should be very unwise to assume that any conditions attested by our private experience alone could safely be applied. Quite apart from the uncertainty of analogical reasoning, we must bear in mind the tremendous realisation which comes in middle age and is expressed by the Chinese poet, "The things I have loved have been different at different times." Our own experience of what is desirable and what is abhorrent is by no means stable even from day to day or from hour to hour. What makes us contented and satisfied at one time will at another be irksome and intolerable. So as far as social science is concerned, we have to recognise that it is limited by the fallibility of the perceptions and inferential powers of the human mind to exactly the same degree as natural science, and does not gain any additional sanction or certainty from the analogy of experience.

What concerns us now is the kind of knowledge we require for the ordering of our own lives and the methods by which this knowledge is to be gained. At the present time what is termed the scientific method enjoys an extraordinary and strange prestige, and many people have come to believe, not only that all necessary knowledge can be gained by scientific methods, but also that any knowledge not so gained is in some way suspect. No such view can stand up to one minute's serious examination, but there is so widespread a belief that problems concerned with the attainment or realisation of values can be solved by the scientific method, that we must give it full consideration. To approach this we must ask ourselves what are the conditions for the acquisition of knowledge.

Reverting to our scale of knowledge, it will be seen that we start with the kind of knowledge that is common to every organised being according to its needs and the nature of its life. The second kind of knowledge is closed to invertebrate animals and to vegetable life, but is open to vertebrates because of the peculiar character of the nervous system they possess. The third kind is closed to the great majority of vertebrate animals, but is open to man on account of the development of his brain, particularly the complex structure of his cerebral hemispheres. This differentiation of possible knowledge suggests the existence of a relation between the kind of knowledge a being can acquire and the level of that being.

I shall use the word "being" as a correlate of knowledge, so we must clarify what we mean by such terms as "being" or "level of being", and "distinctions of being" or "relativity of being". By the word "being", the mode of existence of an organism should be understood, the extent to which it is an integrated whole and can be said to have integrated experience. The vertebrate animal has an integrative mechanism the nervous system—which invertebrate animals and plants do not possess, and this mechanism places the vertebrate on a higher level of being than these other forms of life. Activity, experience and knowledge of higher kinds are, by virtue of this mechanism, accessible to the vertebrates. Man has a still more fully integrated experience and a greater degree of independence of his environment, and so can be said to have more *being* than other forms of organic life. This was discussed earlier, when the question was raised as to how we could determine and be sure that man has, as we believe, a higher level of being. We have seen how we make serious mistakes and overrate the being of man, ascribing to him powers which he does not possess, except in germ or seed form, despite the fact that he has powers which are far greater than those of the rest of the vertebrate animals.

Even when we discount our tendency to exaggerate man's importance and powers, he still remains a being of a very high order compared with the other forms of organic life which inhabit the earth. A very typical and important characteristic of the being of man is that it is not always upon one and the same level. The importance of being awake has already been strongly emphasised. Indeed, we can say that when a man is awake he is on an altogether higher level of being than when he is asleep. When he is awake he has the power of choice and, with it, responsibility. Responsibility is something which we must agree to regard as characterising the level of a being. Perhaps the most certain reason why we place animals on a lower level of being than ourselves is that we do not regard them as responsible for their actions in the same way that men are.

From what has been said about the power of choice, it is clear that even a man cannot be regarded as responsible for his actions unless he is awake, for it is only when he is awake that he enters the realm of values. When he is asleep he may talk and think about values, but they do not actually exist for him in fact, because values exist only when they present themselves in the form of choice between what is better and what is worse, between what is more valuable and what is less valuable.

This leads to the very important conclusion that the level of man's being has the unique quality of depending upon himself, in so far as he has, and does exercise, the power of choice. When he does not choose he lives in a realm without values, where, indeed, he may perform all kinds of remarkable and complicated actions, producing even far-reaching and serious results, but his actions are those of a machine and he cannot be called responsible.

The next question that we have to ask ourselves is whether it is possible for man to attain a still higher level of being than is implied in the condition of being awake and having the power of choice. This brings us to the crux of Part I. Psychological megalanthropism attributes to man a permanent conscious self, the free power of choice and the ability to do effectively what he wants. I have tried to show that none of these attributes can rightly be assigned to people such as we are—you and I and anyone we are likely to meet in the course of our lives. It does not, however, follow that these things cannot be acquired. There is nothing in them which is incompatible with human nature. Although we have many selves, we do not find it difficult to conceive of a man with a single self, free from inward division and conflict, who is the same today and tomorrow and ten years hence. We do not even find it difficult to conceive of a man who at all important and serious moments is awake, and has the power to determine his actions by free choice, with knowledge of what should be done. We can also conceive that a man could acquire the further knowledge which is hidden from us, but which would enable him to act effectively over a period of time and produce results in accordance with his intentions. A man such as this would be on a higher level of being than the highest we can reach. He would have powers and be capable of knowledge greater than anything we possess. We can even suppose that such a man might reach a level of being which would give him not only those powers which we wrongly attribute to ourselves as we are, but further powers, the very possibility of which we do not suspect. With such powers we might associate the ability to reach transcendental knowledge, that is, knowledge which goes beyond anything we can gain through our senses and our minds.

The purpose of this very short description of the being of man has been to convey an idea of the correlation between knowledge and being, of their interdependence, and the fact that on every level of being certain kinds of knowledge are possible and other kinds are not. No indication has been given of the source of knowledge of higher kinds, but I hope we have seen how the scientific method—the work of observation, experiment and inference, based solely on the data of the senses—can give only pragmatic knowledge and that only at its peril does it attempt to deal with questions of value. Although pragmatic knowledge covers an immense field, comprising virtually the whole

of human activity, with all the extraordinary achievements of man, it is still only one stage removed from
animal knowledge. There is nothing derogatory in this
classification of knowledge, for the lower forms of knowledge are, in their way, as valuable and necessary as
the higher, because we obviously could not live at all
without them.[1] What is important is the realisation that
no amount of knowledge of one kind can produce a
grain of knowledge of another kind. Pragmatic knowledge can never disclose value. These two knowledges
are quite distinct from one another. There is danger
of confusing them; but if we do not confuse them, many
things become clear. For instance, it becomes easier to
think about problems of value and problems of fact. In
every situation there is an aspect of fact and an aspect
of value, but however much one knows about the facts
of a situation, not the slightest knowledge of value is
gained. The converse is also true: it is a mistake to
think that judgment of values can add anything to
pragmatic knowledge.

The megalanthropic attitude towards man is based
on his success in dealing with things, upon his pragmatic knowledge, and it fails to take account of his
defective understanding and judgment of values, to say
nothing of his inability to order his life effectively on
the basis of values. We must reject the absurd and

---

[1] Cf. W. R. Sorley, *Moral Values and the Idea of God* (C.U.P., 3rd ed.,
1924), p. 21. ". . . It may be well to banish sternly from our minds the
attitude of moral or aesthetic appreciation when our purpose is simply
to understand the connexions of phenomena."

atrocious attitude to man expressed in Swinburne's "Glory to man in the highest, for man is the master of things". How can the mastery of things entitle us to self-glorification, when it is beyond *things*, in the higher levels of knowledge and the higher levels of being (the possibility of which cannot be denied because we have glimpses of them), that the real meaning of human life, of human purpose, is to be found?

I have tried in these five chapters to introduce the basic material for discussion of the megalanthropic view. The next step is to see how this applies to the present situation in human life, and in Part II we shall be concerned with a positive attitude to the whole of the problem which emerges from this study.

CHAPTER VI

THE END OF AN EPOCH

SO far, we have been trying to survey the prodigious cycle of human experience which has led to the situation in which we find the world today, but instead of discussing only "The Crisis in Human Affairs", which is the subject of this book, we have spent most of our time in trying to make sure that we understand one another. To make sure that people understand one another is a very much bigger undertaking than anyone would believe who had not tried seriously to carry it out. In all that I have put forward I have not tried to convince you of anything, or to prove anything; I have dealt only with statements that are easy to verify or disprove, and left it for you to think about them if you wished to do so. Now that this preparatory work has been done, we can begin to use the language we have been developing to discuss the situation we see around us in the world today.

All over the world people share the feeling that human affairs are passing through a critical or transitional stage. There is a remarkably general agreement both as to the nature of the crisis and the kind of cure it needs. People tend more and more readily to admit that the development of human powers has not been accompanied by any corresponding growth of human wisdom, that our ability to control *things* has outstripped our power to control *ourselves*. The cure proposed usually involves some kind of re-awakening or renewal of spiritual values.

In the case of an organic physical malady, once we have diagnosed the disease and prescribed the remedy we are usually well on the way to curing it; but, with the troubles from which mankind is suffering, things are not taking that course at all. The call for a renewal or revival of values is widespread, but the march of events is in a quite different direction. This, of course, is just what we might have expected to happen as a result of the discrepancy we have noted between human intentions and the outcome of human actions. If we are right in thinking that man cannot *do*, we should not be surprised to find that, although we can see what we ought to do, we fail to do it.

It is a remarkable fact that our intentions are generally good. Generally, perhaps even always, people intend the best, not only for themselves, but also for others; but there is a sad discrepancy between our intentions and our actions, with the consequence that results are usually very different from what we hope for. It is a very dangerous error to overlook or ignore this fact, because to do so gives rise to false judgments about ourselves and our affairs. There is nothing new in the idea that our intentions are generally good, but that the results of our actions do not correspond to them. It was an old, old thought which Samuel Johnson expressed when he said, "Sir, the way to hell is paved with good intentions", and even Johnson did not draw from his observation one very important and necessary conclusion.

We judge not only ourselves, but any group of which we feel ourselves a part, by *intentions*, which we perceive, and not by the outcome of *actions*, which we overlook. We ignore the intentions of other people and groups to which we do not belong, and judge them by their actions and the outcome of their actions. They judge us in the same way, so that we have a situation in which each party can always feel convinced that it is right and the other wrong.

When this contradiction between good intentions, in terms of which we judge ourselves and our own community, and actions and the outcome of actions, by which we judge other people or other communities, arises between individuals or small groups of people, it produces tensions which are seldom resolved without conflict. When larger groups come into contact with one another, and begin to judge themselves in terms of their own intentions and others by their actions, tensions develop on a correspondingly larger scale. When, as at the present time, improved communications result in the groupings of population growing large, and the possibilities of community of sentiment and of collective judgment within groups becomes greater, the danger reaches tragic proportions with great masses of the world's population in violent disagreement, and yet all convinced of their own righteousness.

This kind of situation arises at any period of armed

conflict. During the last war we heard exactly the same sentiments expressed by the speeches or newspapers or radio on the two sides, with exactly the same conviction of rightness on each. This is most striking, and people who are able to be in contact with both sides are always impressed by the massive way in which each overlooks the intentions of the other; it judges itself only by intentions, and the other by actions and the outcome of actions. This is the inevitable result of ignoring the fact that we cannot *do* anything, and that human actions never correspond to intentions. The truth is that no coherent and rational account of the historical process can be given except in terms of the fundamental conclusion that *man cannot do*. Failure to recognise and apply this conclusion is the source of all intolerance and ultimately of suspicion and its outcome in armed conflict.

The distinction between "pragmatic knowledge" and "knowledge of values" is thus an extremely important factor in understanding the present crisis. When we begin to study more deeply we find that pragmatic knowledge is different not only in kind, *but also in origin*, from knowledge of values. Pragmatic knowledge is derived from the analysis and combination of sense data, but knowledge of values cannot be derived from these sources. To illustrate this point let us consider what would happen if we tried to establish a knowledge or system of values solely with the help of the data which our senses can give us, without any reference to our own inner judgments of approval and disapproval.

One example of a value problem will suffice: "When

is the taking of life justified?" In the world around us, among organic beings living on the earth, we see the sway of the law of killing and being killed. Who can kill, kills, and who cannot kill, is eaten. In one form or other throughout organic life we see the survival and success of that which is able to endure. There is nothing to contradict this law except in the relation of parents and offspring or where the ties of blood create an inter-locking of private experience. The more highly organised the form of life, the more do its endurance and survival take a combative and aggressive form, and prevail at the expense of other organisms. Any system of relative values based on this observation would be forced to recognise that the higher the organism the more it destroys, so that the highest law in such a system would be the law of killing. It is quite clear that such a conclusion does not correspond at all to the sense of values we actually have, the dictates of which are far more imperative than judgments based on the data which we can get through our senses, so we must con-clude that our sense of values, our judgments of approval and disapproval, cannot come from the same source as pragmatic knowledge, which is our knowledge of the world in which we live.[1]

[1] This paragraph contains only the sketch of a line of reasoning which requires much fuller development to be convincing. The reader is in-vited to test for himself the conclusion reached when we try to devise a system of values solely from sense experience without any independent "judgment". The idea is not new and has been developed by the Vienna school of philosophy, who wrongly conclude, however, that values are fictitious.

This distinction between pragmatic knowledge and knowledge of values is real and important; but the more we understand, the more certain does it become that peculiar and special difficulties arise in connection with any study of the knowledge of values.

To express knowledge we use language, and language belongs to the domain of the pragmatic. We learn language through our senses, and we employ our bodily organs in producing and in receiving it. This applies even to its interpretation. The meaning of the words we use is very largely derived from our sense experience.

Knowledge of fact changes with time. It can grow or diminish, but it is always subject to the temporal process. Values are not temporal, but eternal. Language, which belongs to pragmatic knowledge, is temporal and changes with the change of knowledge. Values which are eternal do not change, and because they must be clothed in a temporal language, they suffer, *as far as their expression is concerned*, the changes which take place in language by the fact that it belongs to time. This is a very important point and requires careful consideration. There have been times in the history of the world when different languages actually were used for talking about pragmatic knowledge and knowledge of values, but we have now dispensed with this arrangement, and use the same language for both topics.

We are accustomed to regard expression as synonymous with language; but so far as language is concerned we have no means of expressing eternal values except in the words and forms of the ordinary language in which we express temporal truths. This language is not stable, its words have a different meaning today both from that which they had 100 or 1,000 years ago and from that which they will have in the future. People notice this, and declare that truth perishes. They say, "The truth of today is the falsehood of tomorrow and the truth of yesterday is the falsehood of today", but, as Bacon says in his essay on Friendship, "It had beene hard for him that spake it to have put more Truth and untruth together in a few words", because truth, which belongs to value, is eternal, and does not change, although the expression of truth depends on language, which is temporal. So it is quite right and justifiable to say the *expression* of truth which is valid today becomes invalid tomorrow. We are thus confronted with the difficulty that, whereas we human beings have something in us which can apprehend eternal values, we have no means of expressing these values except in temporal language.

Men try to overcome this difficulty in various ways. One is to use a symbolism which by its nature is not temporal, for in symbolical language a symbol can be chosen to convey an eternal meaning. The Chinese word Tao, for example, to which Taoist writers in all good periods have carefully abstained from giving any verbal meaning or interpretation, remains permanently a symbol of transcendental experience. The Cross in Christianity is an eternal symbol which does not change in meaning with the change of language. It is when we attempt to interpret and talk about symbols that we fall back into the same difficulty as before, because the language we use has a changing character. The same applies to the expression of eternal values in works of art. Art is a timeless activity; but the interpretation of art, the translation of artistic expression into mental concepts, is as much subject to the temporal as any other verbal form. Nevertheless the role of Art in the expression of value situations is so important that we shall consider it more fully at a later stage. For the present we are concerned with the essentially transient character of verbal meanings.

We can try to overcome this transcience by taking steps to bring language up to date. A certain group of Eternal Values was expressed in a particular form of language 2,000 years ago. That language was inevitably borrowed from the pragmatic knowledge of the time, because there was no other way of conveying the meaning of these values to those people to whom they were not directly apparent as a matter of their own inward experience.[1] Whatever precautions are taken, this necessity of conveying meaning in language which derives from the contemporary pragmatic knowledge must result in compromise for which, in the long run, the price must be paid. An attempt may be made either to re-state the same truths by a modification or modernisation of the old language, or to make a completely fresh start and follow the line of expressing what appear to be new truths in the language of the current period. These two ways roughly approximate

[1] Cf. Matt. xiii. 17, 34, 35, 54.

to the way of the Reformation and the way of the Renaissance.

If we think of Western history, leaving the inward or experienced aspect of the Reformation out of account, and thinking only in terms of the attempts which have been made to express a certain group of eternal values in language which has been brought up to date, the difficulties become increasingly acute with the advance of pragmatic knowledge. The set of values of which we speak was formulated at a time when it appeared, as far as contemporary pragmatic knowledge went, that the earth was the centre of the universe, and man a special creation, standing apart from the rest of organic beings. It could therefore appear that human experience should occupy a central place in any attempt to understand the universe. God and man could seem the only leading actors on the stage. The progress of science—the particular form of pragmatic knowledge which influences language—has now shattered all such conceptions. We can no longer think of the earth as being in any sense the centre of the universe. On the contrary, we now recognise that the universe is vastly greater than anything our minds can conceive, and that the possible experiences of values which reside in it infinitely transcend anything we can hope to understand. Moreover, as far as physical and astronomical science are concerned, we are forced to accept the invalidation of almost all the meaning of the language which people have spoken for thousands of years, and which they still speak today—especially when we are

121

dealing with a vast expanse of space and time and magnitudes ranging from spiral nebulae to atoms.

Biological science also forces us to the conclusion that we cannot look on man as a specially favoured being in a position of private importance in the life of the earth. We have now to accept the fact that man enters into the life of the earth and is related to other organised beings in a quite different way from that in which he appeared to be only a few generations ago. Even more serious and greater difficulties come from the development of genetic science, of embryology, of our knowledge of the influence of diet on human behaviour, of experimental psychology, of endocrinology and other branches of physiological and biological science. These developments force us to abandon age-old conceptions of human responsibility and the independence of behaviour from physical causes. I should recommend to anyone who is not familiar with these developments the study of papers in medical journals which show how organic lesions, dietetic disturbances, derangement of the endocrine system, and other physical factors can alter the psychological life of individuals and affect their power of choice, their behaviour and what used to be called "moral character". This new knowledge compels us to abandon or modify the meanings we have been accustomed to attach for many generations to some of the most important words which we use for expressing knowledge of values.

Little by little we have abandoned the meaning of words like "individual", "person", "soul", "sin", "moral responsibility". Their meaning has now to be entirely reconstructed, because we cannot ignore the effect on language of changes of pragmatic knowledge. The changes in meaning are so great that it is virtually impossible to succeed with any simple reconstruction or modernisation of language on Reformation lines.

The alternative course is the Renaissance method, but this leads to even greater confusion and worse disaster, for it abandons the conception of eternal values altogether, and substitutes pragmatic pseudo-values. The actual words that belong to the Renaissance system of values are most misleading. One of the main political achievements of the Renaissance—the French Revolution—was founded on Liberty, Equality and Fraternity. Fraternity can be left out of account from the start, because it soon disappeared except for the common sonship of all men to *la Mère Guillotine*. Liberty and Equality appeared to be sound, useful, valuable words, but what do they mean today? In one great nation the pursuit of liberty is leading to an increasingly severe degree of suppression of equality; in another the slow progress of equality is offset by the gradual loss of liberty, and in yet another both liberty and equality are condemned as counter-revolutionary tendencies. Lord Acton, the great historian of liberty, who spent fifty years preparing material for a history of liberty which was never written, came at last to the simple conclusion that liberty is incompatible with equality.

The system of pragmatic values which grew out of

the Renaissance, and which has external manifestations in English utilitarianism or possibly in the Marx–Engels theories, proves on examination to be simply a substitute system in which invented or pseudo-values are used instead of eternal values; all true values are either left out or hopelessly distorted.

This is a very serious state of affairs, because human beings not only should, but in fact they do, act upon their sense of values. All the time we, and other people, are influenced by the distinction of what matters and what does not matter, whether this is expressed in a formulated value system or whether it is merely felt. When people become confused and bewildered in their systems of values, they also become confused and bewildered in their actions. We are just reaching the end of a period during which hopes were placed upon the pseudo-values of the Renaissance, and nothing is arising to take their place. At the same time an increasing strain is placed on mankind, a growing tension, arising from the ever-growing scale of the contradiction between our own intentions, by which we judge ourselves, and actions, by which we judge others. This results in a growing weariness and indifference, which come from the lack of any accepted system of those values on which action depends. To feel that there is a reason for living is, in the last analysis, the most important thing in life. It is on this most important subject that we are most wretchedly uncertain and confused today.

We are forced to these conclusions when we look at

124

the world and apply to it the tests which we have been discussing: tests of what is real and what is illusory in human life, the test of the distinction between knowledge by which we know facts—*pragmatic knowledge*—and knowledge by which we act—*knowledge of values*.

We can also see that this state of affairs arises at every point from an over-emphasis on the importance and power of man, an excessive confidence in his ability to know and to *do*. Because we think we can *do*, and refuse to accept the fact that everything happens to us without reference to our intentions and that we can do nothing, we turn our backs on the discrepancy between good intentions and our failure to carry them out. Because we think that man is the measure of things, we trust our pragmatic knowledge, and so sin against the unchanging eternal value system. We prostitute it by attempting to put it into the inappropriate language which has developed through the advance of pragmatic knowledge. This involves acceptance of the successive compromises that have been made one after another in the statement and expression of eternal values in philosophy and religion. In following this course we have come to trust unduly in human knowledge and understanding, believing that from advancing pragmatic knowledge we can distil a system of values upon which we can rely. This is why I have called this present time the Megalanthropic Epoch, and why the title of this chapter might also have been "The Root Cause of the Present Crisis", or the failure of megalanthropic values.

We have seen how the megalanthropic revolution 2,500 years ago initiated an epoch which emphasised the value and importance of the individual. This change of emphasis provided a great and important new element in human life, and resulted in a strong upward surge in human experience; but although it was creative in its origin, it has become destructive in its end. We have a new lesson to learn—the lesson of humility, the most difficult of all lessons. We talk glibly about humility, but to practise it is the most difficult of all disciplines. To become humble about man would mean accepting the fact that we are not free beings, able to choose, that we are not effective beings, able to do, and that we are not important beings, the centre of the universe, as each man really at the bottom of his heart feels himself to be, but unimportant and ineffectual.

To accept these truths would mean casting aside far more than people are prepared to dispense with, and this applies just as much to religious leaders and philosophers and those we may call the professional "good people" as to all those who are merely full of good intentions. All the politicians, soldiers, great leaders of industry and of labour are equally permeated with the megalanthropic error. Even the present difficulties of mankind are far from being a writing on the wall sufficiently menacing to prepare people to think differently.

I remember words which were spoken to me many years ago by a very wise and sensible man, from whom I learned many things. He said, "You want the truth.

Well, if you want the truth, you must be prepared to throw everything into the fire. Truth is like gold, it will survive the fire, so if you have any gold it will come out of the fire; if you have not, then everything will be burnt; but you must be prepared for that."

If we are to continue this study, we must think about the consequences of this challenge. We must try to learn how to look at our own individual lives and at human affairs, at our aims and purposes, the kind of happiness to which we should aspire, and the ways by which we should hope to attain it.

It is my belief that in coming to the decision that the megalanthropic standpoint must be abandoned we are merely anticipating the inevitable consequence of the present world situation. Sooner or later—very probably within the lifetime of most of us—the present epoch will come grindingly or crashingly to a standstill. World institutions, national institutions, all the manifestations of megalanthropic society will demonstrate by their failure the rottenness of their foundations. Then, and then only, will the ground be prepared for a fresh harvest of enlightenment and expansion based upon a more fundamental humility than mankind has known in all the long ages of recorded history. In Part II, I shall try to show you what the seeds of that harvest are like and to draw your attention to encouraging indications that their sowing has already begun.

Part II

THE COMING OF THE NEW EPOCH

CHAPTER VII

PSYCHO-STATIC AND PSYCHO-KINETIC DOCTRINES

SO far we have taken for granted that we are witnessing a Crisis in Human Affairs, but we have not yet considered why the present state of tension in the world must be regarded as something different from the tensions which throughout the epoch have always arisen both within and between communities and have resolved themselves by conflicts, small or large. Before we could do this it was necessary to see how the world has reached its present condition. We have found that the root cause has been the gradual acceptance of a megalanthropic attitude to man. Our examination of this attitude has led to a survey of some of the causes of the present crisis, or state of tension, and anyone who has thought about them will have seen that they do give a special significance to the present time.

We have before us two tendencies which make for critical and dangerous situations in human life. The first is our proneness to judge ourselves by our intentions and others by their actions. This leads to states of tension. The second leads to states of depression and inertia because, when men's values become confused, their actions become confused also, and they grow weary and apathetic. At the root of both these tendencies

131

we discover megalanthropism—the tendency to over-rate the importance of man and to exaggerate his powers and capacities. The evils which are commonly discerned in modern life—the idolisation of the State, the loss of personal liberty, the failure of religion added to the fear and suspicion of the future which have always haunted mankind—are merely symptoms of the underlying malady. The physician recognises the transition from the chronic infection to the acute condition. This is characterised by a sharp change of tempo, when it soon becomes clear whether the outcome will be collapse or recovery. The change of tempo and other symptoms of the acute crisis are unmistakably with us today.

What are to be our reactions to this tremendous situation? We should begin by understanding that it is not the existence of a crisis only that makes it important, or even necessary, to think about the human problem today. There is a perennial human problem which exists apart from the recurrence of crises and tensions and weariness. It is only for very short periods of time, and then only in very small communities or among privileged classes within a community, that there is ever any sense that the millennium has arrived, or any desire that the existing state of affairs should continue indefinitely. A general sense of dissatisfaction with the state of human life and a desire that things should be different are quite usual, and although they naturally become acute in times of crisis, their presence is characteristic of human nature. There are two

132

distinct ways in which we can conceive the possibility of setting the situation to rights.

The first is to regard the essential human nature as something given, and the solution of the problem as a change in the relation of man to his environment. This we shall call the "psycho-static" view, according to which the *psyche*, or essential nature of man, is unchangeable, and the solution of his problems can be sought only in some new relation to his environment generally, some new relation both to the community in which he lives and to his fellow-men. The alternative we shall call the "psycho-kinetic" view, which asserts the possibility of movement or transformation within man's psyche or essential nature. These two views lead us to think about adaptation to the circumstances of life in terms of either external or internal changes. The psycho-static view implies that man's essential nature must remain static, or stationary, and the psycho-kinetic that his psyche, or essential nature, can change.

We must first decide what it is we mean by man's psyche, or essential nature. His body, his mind, his physical or his mental powers are not at any given moment his psyche. We all know that we are born with small and feeble bodies, which grow and mature, acquiring powers which are absent at birth. In the new-born child the mental powers are not active, and do not begin to be active for several years. They usually mature and reach their greatest strength and flowering at a later age than the body. Apart from our physical and mental powers, we have experience, knowledge of the world and capacity for making judgments. All these develop at different rates, and reach maturity at different times. Later they begin to diminish and withdraw, until inevitably, unless cut off by premature death, they come to old age and final dissolution. This cycle of birth, growth, maturity, decline, old age and death is a part of the essential human nature. It is something, moreover, that we share not only with other men, but with everything we see in the world around us. Everything that exists in time is under the law of this cycle. We are not entitled to isolate one fraction—the period of growth to maturity—and regard it as constituting a change in man's essential nature. It is just as much a part of our essential nature that after maturity is reached decline should set in. The "psycho-kinetic" view of man refers to changes other than his capacity for maturing in the sense of development of his physical or mental powers, or even his capacity for judgment. The acceptance of these latter facts is common both to the psycho-static and the psycho-kinetic views.

It is also very important not to confuse the psycho-kinetic view with "evolution doctrines". During the past 100 years the doctrine of biological evolution has been very widely accepted, and man, in common with other beings living on the earth, is regarded as having evolved from lower, or at any rate simpler, forms, and so may be expected to evolve into higher or more complex forms. This process, if it can be rightly applied

134

to man, involves a slow change in which the individual is passive, and it is because the individual is short-lived and feeble in relation to his environment that the mechanism of evolution or natural selection is presumed to act. At any given moment, however, the essential nature of man is regarded as stable, and the change, if any, is presumed to occur over long periods of time.

It would, of course, be possible to regard the evolutionary sequence as providing a means of determining direction, so that we could find value in evolution from lower to higher, from simpler to more complex forms, and accept the evolutionary doctrine of value which was widely held in the last century. We could think, like Tennyson, of "waxing tree and waning leaf", or of Nature saying, with George Meredith, to man, "Live in your offspring as I live in mine". Such a view regards man as the passive element in a process which goes very slowly and almost in spite of him.

There are also doctrines according to which evolution is either purposive, and even divinely directed, as proposed by some modern Christian apologists, or without purpose and proceeding by blind conflict, as suggested by dialectical materialism; but in all its forms the evolutionary doctrine regards man, the individual, as passive in relation to a great secular process, occurring over long periods of time, which at any given moment leaves his essential nature unchanged. Such doctrines as these belong to the psycho-static view.

There is still one more point to be made clear about the distinction between the psycho-static and psycho-kinetic views. So far we have spoken only about human life as we know it, from birth through growth, maturity, and decline to old age and dissolution. Men in all conditions of life and over long periods of time have entertained and do entertain beliefs about survival, after the death of the body. Survival doctrines are not necessarily psycho-kinetic. On the contrary, the survival beliefs of the great majority of mankind, both in the West, where they have been associated with reward and punishment, heaven and hell, and in the East, where they are connected with reincarnation doctrines of repeated lives, are all held in forms in which the presumed survival is a continuation of the same kind of experience as exists in life. The interpretation of this doctrine can vary between wide extremes, from the simple reappearance of the body, complete with all its accustomed equipment, in some islands of the blest, to resurrection and survival in an earthly paradise or translation to some supraterrestrial or disembodied existence. The form does not matter. So long as experience "beyond the grave" is conceived as analogous to the experience of life, the doctrines belong to the psycho-static view.

The distinction between psycho-static and psycho-kinetic is not a distinction between religious and secular or non-religious conceptions. Religious doctrines can be, and many are, psycho-static. In notions of reward and punishment we make use of conceptions of right

136

and wrong, pleasure and pain, which are based on our essential nature as it is, and in so far as we project these notions out of this life into another—thinking of rewards as somehow corresponding to what we should call pleasant and desirable things in this life, and punishments as corresponding to what we should call painful and undesirable experiences in this life—we assume a continuity or sameness of the essential nature of man, which necessarily brings the doctrine into the psycho-static group.

Religious doctrines can be psycho-static in one of two ways. They can be expressed in language corresponding to our ordinary pragmatic language, making use of ideas derived from sense experience and thoughts. Their value system thus comes to be based upon human experience, and religion becomes, in effect, humanitarianism. The criteria of right and wrong are derived from what the religious dogmatist has come to know and understand of essential human nature and of the human psyche, through applying to their study the same methods that he would use for acquiring pragmatic knowledge. All such forms of religion must be psycho-static, because they start from human nature as it is and make no allowances for the possibility that it may change. Alternatively, we can have simple ritualistic religions, and the religions of good works, based on the notions of reward and punishment which we have already discussed or upon obligations towards God derived from our traditional or habitual conceptions of obligations towards a human father or tribal

137

chief. Values translated into such terms become temporal in character. Reward or punishment is thought of in a way that implies a temporal sequence of experience, corresponding to the ordinary process of our sense perceptions and mental operations. In order to understand the power of psycho-kinetic religion, we must steep ourselves in the writings of a man like St. Paul, for whom the very meaning of the religious life is the dying and being born again in Christ.[1] The change in the essential nature of man which is symbolised in this death and rebirth takes place, not in another world, but "here in this very life". It is an eternal transformation and not a temporal process. Through it, a man becomes concretely what he always has been in potency. This is the root of the Psycho-kinetic Doctrine and without it any religious teaching remains on the psycho-static level.

If we took the view, as we might well do, that all essentially religious doctrines must be psycho-kinetic, and demand a change in the essential nature of man, we should have to dismiss as secular much that passes for religion today. At the same time it is clear that the idea that man's essential nature must change occupies a central place in the origin of the great religions. The Christian religion is based on the doctrine that men must be born again, or die and rise with Christ. The conception of the "twice-born" is the central teaching of Buddhism and all the great religions of India. It

[1] Cf. Albert Schweitzer, *The Mysticism of Paul the Apostle* (A. & C. Black, 1931).

138

is in the subsequent development and expansion of religions that a progressive tendency towards psycho-static notions appears. The cause of this tendency can be fully understood only by seeing clearly what is meant by the psycho-kinetic doctrine of man.

The real purpose of Part I was to lay bare the true character of this doctrine and to show how, by observation and analysis, we can establish that man misunderstands and exaggerates his own essential nature and overestimates his powers. If we once accept the conclusion that the true nature of man is that he is not one, but a multiplicity, that he is asleep and that he cannot do, and that he is a machine, then one thing at least can be said about the psycho-kinetic view—it implies the possibility of remedying these defects. We can think of man—who is now, as we know him, not one but many and inwardly discordant—becoming united and harmonious within himself; man who is now asleep, and to whom things happen without choice, waking up and acquiring the power to choose; man who does not know himself or the world or the way in which things happen, learning to know these things and to choose wisely and effectively, and so to achieve purposes of abiding importance. Such a transformation would constitute a psycho-kinetic change; but this is only one aspect of the problem, and it is with the second aspect that the difficulty begins.

When we speak about the essential nature of man, we mean man such as we know him or, better, such as we can know him. If we could shed our illusions about man and look at him with open eyes we should see him as a particular kind of being, occupying a definite position in the whole scale of existence, which ranges from All to Nothing. Now, it is an essential characteristic of being that no-one can perceive a higher level than his own. We can perhaps feel, and even be confident, that it exists; but we cannot perceive or participate in it, because to participate in it we should have to be on the same level, and that would mean that our own being had changed. Therefore, if the psycho-kinetic view of man implies a change of level of being, it involves a change from something which we do and can know, to something which we do not and cannot know.

To perceive the goal towards which such a change in man's essential nature is directed, we should need transcendental knowledge—knowledge which goes beyond our present possibilities. The essential character of transcendental knowledge is that it refers not to what we are, but to what we might be. But we lack the means of expressing it, for if we found the pragmatic language of our ordinary experience inadequate for expressing judgment of values, it must be much more inadequate for expressing transcendental knowledge. If we wish to speak about transcendental experience, we are faced with a dilemma; either we must use a symbolism which is incomprehensible, or we must borrow our language, that is, our ideas, similes and illustrations, from our ordinary experience; but as our ordinary experience is confined to time-like things, the gap between the known and the unknown still remains unbridged.

It appears, therefore, that the nature of the goal implied in the psycho-kinetic doctrine must be unknown and unknowable. We are now confronted with the central problem of all religious and philosophical doctrines which attempt to deal with the possibility of changing man's essential nature. When, in the Gospels, we read "Except a man be born again", we ask with Nicodemus, "How can a man be born when he is old?" Whatever language men may use for describing psycho-kinetic doctrines, they always meet with the same difficulty. Similes are chosen perforce from our everyday pragmatic language; we can only fix on the meaning which those similes have for us, and do not see the meaning towards which they are trying to point, so we dispute and argue about the outward sign and miss the inward grace. If, then, there is no means of approaching the psycho-kinetic doctrine except by a mortal jump into the unknown, with nothing but a blind faith to rely on, it appears that in order to discuss it we shall have to depart from our original principle of speaking only about facts. Nevertheless, I am going to try to convey to you in the next few chapters something about the transcendental aspect of the psycho-kinetic doctrine and hope, without asking you to make the leap into the unknown, to give you some idea of how man's essential nature can change.

There are certain immediate indications which can show at least something of the character of the change which is possible in man's essential nature. These indications arise from the fact that man's nature is not stable and unvarying, but undergoes great fluctuations between extreme despondency and what is almost worse, a state of mere blind satisfaction with ourselves and our activities, or just complete immersion in activity when no thought of discrimination is present at all. Among all these fluctuations we sometimes come upon moments of inner peace, when we know things differently, and there are also moments of similar value but quite different character, when we know the excitement of participation in beauty, with knowledge, with understanding and with insight. Between these and our worst moments there is a whole gamut of experiences, duller or more vivid, with less sense of existence and value or with greater sense of existence and value, through which we find ourselves fluctuating incessantly.

Together with these fluctuations we also find, if we care to verify it, that we have a limited power of choice, different from the imaginary power of choice which people ascribe to themselves without testing it or knowing what it means : a real power of choice, a real power of standing apart from ourselves and saying "yes" or "no" to our own activities. We can verify the existence in us of a real power to say yes and no, and because of these two things—the fluctuations of our state and the possession of a real if limited power of choice—we can say that if we only knew how, we could strengthen the higher and better states and weaken or even banish the worse and lower states. A realisation of this kind is a concrete indication that it is possible to bring about a change which would in fact be a change in our essential nature.

Let us pause to look more closely at this phrase, "change in our essential nature". There is a grave risk that it may be interpreted in too temporal, too pragmatic a sense, associated with the acquisition of powers, knowledge, abilities and skills of various kinds; but these are not the changes to which I refer. The true meaning of the phrase was implicit in the Greek Mysteries, in which the inner life of man was taken to be analogous to the harvest. Man himself was conceived as a grain, which could die as a grain but be reborn as a plant, different from the grain. A bushel of wheat has two possible destinies: one, in which it is ground and made into flour and becomes bread, and another, in which it is sown in the ground, germinates and, becoming a plant, gives a hundred grains for one that was sown. This idea was borrowed by St. Paul in describing the resurrection, where he says, "Thou fool, that which thou sowest is not quickened except it die . . .". "It is sown a natural body, it is raised a spiritual body." These illustrations show that the change referred to is not a difference in the use to which a substance is put, but a transformation of the very substance itself. Many have sought to express the idea that man is not a complete, final being, but a being in whose own hands it lies to transform himself. This is a very hard notion to convey, but it is the

143

essence of the psycho-kinetic doctrine. In order to understand it better, we must have a clear idea of the distinction between time and eternity. I propose, therefore, to discuss this in the next chapter, as everything I want to say about the psycho-static and pyscho-kinetic views can be conveyed adequately only if we have some idea of the nature of our existence in time and in eternity, and how the two are necessary to one another.[1]

[1] Cf. Albert Schweitzer, *op. cit.*, p. 99. ". . . He who has the true knowledge can be conscious of himself as at one and the same time in the transient world an d the eternal world." Schweitzer rightly emphasises the impor tance of the eschatological basis of St. Paul's mysticism, but does not see that the coexistence of worlds on different levels must have been present to the apostle in a passage such as 2 Cor. xii. 2.

CHAPTER VIII

TIME AND ETERNITY

THE subject of our discussion in this chapter is the most difficult and, in some ways, the most important in our whole programme. I want to put before you a new approach to the problem of time and eternity, and the possibility which this presents of finding a link between pragmatic knowledge, transcendental knowledge and knowledge of values.

We must start by casting our minds rapidly over the progress of natural science during the past two centuries. The simple mechanical universe which appeared adequate to the mathematical physicists of the eighteenth century has given place to a much more complicated conception, of which general relativity and quantum mechanics are typical manifestations. These new physical theories involve a far greater departure from the ordinary way of thinking about the world than most people imagine. They have undermined the categories of thought which, in the days of Kant and Hegel, seemed to be unshakeable, ultimate truths. We can no longer speak of space and time as absolute, causality as unambiguous, or even the laws of logic as simple and ultimate.

In much the same way, the progress of biological science has undermined the simple mechanistic views

K   145 of living organisms which were considered adequate by the thought of the eighteenth century, but although biology was making important progress in its own field, it contributed very little to the construction of systems of thought, and it happened that the great leaders of thought at that time were themselves physical scientists.[1] Consequently, the philosophers, influenced as they were by the dominance of physical science, tended to accept mechanistic explanations of the universe, founded on simple causality, and the belief that any process can be explained entirely from behind forwards, from past to future. La Place, for example, suggested that if we could know exactly the state of the world at a given moment, this knowledge, coupled with knowledge of all the laws of motion, would enable us to predict exactly the state of the world at any given future moment. This is the essence of the mechanistic view of the universe as expressed by, say, Bertrand Russell today.

The status of biological science has fundamentally changed within the last sixty or seventy years. It has begun to establish facts which are at variance with the simple mechanistic view of organic beings. Many biologists have come to recognise that we cannot understand anything about organic beings unless we take into account a certain directiveness, which we may call by the name of purpose, and which is diametrically opposed to any mechanistic explanation, for it relates

[1] See the interesting discussion of this point by A. N. Whitehead in *Science and the Modern World*, Chapter IV.

146

the activity of animals to some need to be served or some end to be gained. It is impossible, in any discussion of the behaviour of living organisms, to avoid using words and methods of description which have a directive form, implying that something is done for some reason. This is extremely awkward for those who assert that in the long run all descriptions and explanations must be reduced to causal terms, *i.e.* without any reference to the future.

These tendencies, which destroy the coherence of the categories of the eighteenth-century thought, have brought about a collapse of the structure of the pragmatic knowledge which has been built up in the last three centuries. There is no longer any convincing, unified way of thinking about either Nature or the world of inward experience. We have, on the one hand, the progressively accelerating accumulation of exact detailed and useful knowledge [1] in almost every field of activity of natural science and, on the other, a greater and greater tendency for the various fields of investigation to be isolated. This peculiar tendency towards intensive specialisation and the vast increase of knowledge it brings, contrasted with the inability to construct or retain any sort of unified conception of the world which natural science studies, has led to a general feeling of expectancy, which we can trace both in the history of science and in books written about scientific knowledge at the present time. It is constantly suggested

[1] Not mere information, but knowledge how to do many things: the knowledge of *homo faber*.

147

that some new way of thinking is about to emerge and break down the isolation between the different fields of science, each of which is proving so successful only so long as it narrows down its field of studies.

A similar expectancy prevails in the domain of transcendental knowledge. I have spoken already of the general tendency to assert that, unless mankind can re-establish ultimate values in some convincing form, we cannot avoid some great disaster. The realisation of the urgency of the problem leads naturally to the hope that some new way of expressing ultimate values must and will be found.

It is the prevalence of this mood of expectancy that gives such crucial importance to our present studies. A new understanding of time and eternity can provide, on the one hand, a uniting power in the domain of pragmatic knowledge, and, on the other, a language in which ultimate truths can be expressed in a form which is comprehensible to modern Western thought. It is of course impossible, in the space at our disposal, to give more than an indication of the facts on which such new understanding can be based. To cover even that amount of ground will inevitably necessitate the sacrifice of a certain amount of exactness and completeness. It should, however, be possible to establish a certain line of thought and make its significance clear.

Let us start by thinking about time. Time is characterised by successiveness, irreversibility and transcience or impermanence. All events which occur in time show these characteristics. No special research is

148

required to discover them; they are immediate deliveries of all human experience. They present themselves to all men at all times, and the more acute and sensitive the perception, the more do the qualities of successiveness, irreversibility and impermanence of time impress themselves. The great poets in every age and language have always been seized with a sense of the perishability of all things that are in time.

> "Si notre vie est moins qu'une journée
> En l'éternel, si l'an qui fait le tour
> Chasse nos jours sans espoir de retour,
> Si périssable est toute chose née,
> Que songes-tu, mon âme emprisonnée?
> Pourquoi te plaît l'obscur de notre jour?"

The last century saw the discovery of an exact numerical expression for that perishability of time which John Locke called "the perpetual perishing of duration". The Second Law of Thermodynamics states that in every process in which an exchange of energy is involved, the quality of the energy at the end of the process is lower than it was at the beginning. The same principle was later expressed in another form by Boltzmann when he said that the passage of time always produced a tendency for systems to pass to more and more probable states. From that came the notion, first formulated by Lord Kelvin, of the inevitable running down of the universe by the passage of all matter towards states in which there is less and less likelihood that anything new will happen, so that everything will fall at length into a perpetual sameness, from which no further change will be possible.

149

Bertrand Russell, in a marvellous piece of writing in *The Philosophy of a Rationalist*, concludes that the only thing which beseems a man in face of the inevitable perishing of all things around him is to have the courage to accept the facts and live with the certainty that everything must fail and fall into decay. But there is something in us which revolts against this conclusion. To most of us it is quite unacceptable, *in spite of the fact that it accords with our immediate experience.*

The mathematical physicists were not the first teachers of the doctrine that everything wears away. One of the most famous sayings of Gotama Buddha is, " Impermanent are all component things. Whatsoever comes into existence bears within it the seeds of its own dissolution." In one of the greatest religious poems in the world, the "Maitri Upanishad," which is probably even older than the Buddhist scriptures, when Brihadratha, the king who forsook the world to search for permanence, meets the sage Shakâyanya, he asks:

"Lord, in this wretched perishable body, a transient compound of mere matter, what is the good of enjoyment of desires? In this state, in which we are afflicted by desire, anger, greed, delusion, fear, despondency, envy, separation from what we love, union with what we hate, hunger, thirst, old age, death, disease and sorrow—all the ills of mortal life—what good can be found in desires which perish?

"Everything that lives on earth grows old, insects

and animals, the grass and the trees, all arise, decay and perish.

"But what indeed of these? There are others greater: warriors, kings and rulers of the world. In spite of all their glory, they went forth from this world into that.

"But what indeed of these? There are others greater. There is the drying up of oceans, the falling away of mountains, the deviation of the fixed Pole Star, the dissolution of the Galaxy, the retreat of the Celestial Bodies from their station. In this world of unending change, what is the good of enjoyment of desires? When he has tasted them a man returns again and again here to earth.

"Be pleased to deliver me. In this wheel of existence, I am like a frog imprisoned in a dried up well. Lord, thou art my way of escape, thou alone art my way of escape."

Lord Kelvin was anticipated by 2,500 years!

Modern Western man thinks, or used to think, that the way of escape was to be found in doctrines of evolution and progress, in the idea that there is an advancing tide, which, although itself a process in time, can still defy the fundamental laws of time and so absolve us from accepting the pessimistic conclusions forced upon us by the laws of physical science. Such specious doctrines can lead only to confusion and contradiction. We have already noted the modern tendency to mistake one stage in a cyclic process for a secular process, continuing in a positive direction, but we are bound to admit that we have no evidence of anything which we may call progress at the present time—or, if we choose to believe that what is going on in the world today is progress, we have no evidence which justifies the belief that this process will not in its turn lose momentum, and fall away and perish as all progressive movements in the life of mankind have done in the past. We cannot possibly justify any feeling of confidence that what has in the past always been a cycle of rise and fall has now, for no assignable reason, become a movement of continuous advance.

If we look more closely into the question of whether or not there can be, *in time*, at once the general character of successiveness, irreversibility and impermanence, and the operation of a forward, upward, expanding and progressive process, we must see that if both exist, one and the same mechanism cannot be responsible for the two. That is all we require to establish at this stage. If we know from physical science that the temporal process is characterised by the running down which we call the Second Law of Thermodynamics, and if we find this is operative everywhere, both in living organisms and in inanimate matter, we can suppose only, either that there is some inherent contradiction in time, or that our inward belief that this cannot be the whole character of the world must be founded on something other than time alone.

If we cannot believe that the only meaning of life is that it has no meaning, we cannot look for meaning in

152

the temporal process unless we ascribe to it an inherent contradiction which would make it nonsensical. This aspect of the problem needs particular stress because, unless it is quite clear, it will not be possible to make the next step, which is to ask ourselves how it is that we "know" that everything runs down. The answer is that we know this, as we know everything else about the external world, through our senses.

Our senses are physical instruments. This is now fairly well understood. Our eyes work by a transforma-tion of electromagnetic energy, our ears by a trans-formation of the vibrational energy in the air; our sense of taste and smell work by transformations of chemical energy, and it is by a transformation of mechanical energy that we touch and feel. All our sense perceptions depend on transformations of energy, but, as transformations of energy are the very field in which the Second Law of Thermodynamics has been established, it is not surprising that our senses should give us data which exemplify this law.[1] Our mental processes, our thinking, our manipulation of words and signs, which involve the operation of the central nervous system, act in the same way. In the West we are accustomed to talk about "the five senses", and to regard the senses as different from our minds, but in Hindu psychological systems they speak of six senses—these five and the inner sense, the *antahkarana*, which is the manipulation of words and signs. This inward working also depends on energy transformation,

[1] Cf. A. R. Ubbelohde, *Time and Thermodynamics* (Oxford, 1947).

and it is therefore natural, almost inevitable, that, like the others, it should give results which are characteristic of all energy interchanges. On examination it becomes clear that all our knowledge about the running down of things comes from our sense perceptions and the working of our central nervous system.

Now, we must ask ourselves one thing more. Do we find anything in our own experience which is exempt from this running down? Can we detect any process which need not obey the Second Law of Thermodynamics? Most of you will have studied simple dynamics at school, and will have been taught that when a pendulum is in motion two kinds of energy are present. When the bob is in full motion, it can knock things out of its way, or, as we say, "do work" by its *kinetic energy*. When the pendulum rises (you can see this best when it has a long shaft), it gradually comes to a standstill at the end of its swing. For a moment it is stationary—all visible movement has disappeared; the energy which could do visible work while it was moving has turned into *potential energy*, which cannot be seen. The interesting thing about potentital energy is that it is exempt from running down or decay. A rock may remain for centuries at the top of a mountain. During all that time its potentiality for falling is stored up undiminished. When it begins to move, it develops great energy of motion, or kinetic energy, as it crashes down the mountain-side; but finally all this disappears into movement of the air and heat of the earth. Again, I may have a book on my shelves which I do not touch for months or years; but all the time the potential energy which would enable that book to fall to the ground and hit the floor remains undiminished. Rest is as much a fact as motion, and it teaches us that a form of energy exists, in "stored-up" possibilities, which is not subject to the decay of time.

Let us consider a different example. I have already spoken about the impossibility of even thinking about living processes without using words which imply direction and purpose, aim and end. This is strikingly discussed in *The Directiveness of Organic Activities* by Professor E. S. Russell. I should advise anyone who is in any doubt to read it, but I do not think the majority of people require convincing that an organism acts in fulfilment of needs. Nevertheless, even professional biologists often do not realise what a difficult idea is involved when purpose or the fulfilment of needs is spoken of in relation to beings which are certainly unable to foresee the future, and almost certainly unaware even of the present. Even the simplest organisms, such as the amoeba, or the small organisms of our own bodies, like the white corpuscles of our blood, all act unmistakably *towards* ends which they cannot know. We are therefore faced with the fact that there is in a living organism an unexplained source of activity. It is meaningless to say that the future beckons to it and makes it act in a certain way. It is equally absurd to try to define ends without reference to the future, as we should have to do if we were to say that

155

the activity of the organism emerges mechanically out of its past. Nor can we think of the organism as aware of the present and adapting its activity to the immediate situation. Living organisms can be said to have *ends without aims*.

It would be both interesting and helpful to study the activity of a certain worm described by E. S. Russell, the paramoecium, which absorbs different parts of the hydra to make up for something which it lacks itself. This, and countless other examples of directiveness without purpose, are quite impossible to describe, let alone explain, without the notion of some underlying pattern which cannot without contradiction be placed in the past, or in the present, or in the future. So we have to think of organic activity as another example of something which does not fit into and cannot be explained in terms of the successiveness of time. In the pendulum we found something which escapes from the running down and transience of time; in living organisms there is something which escapes from successiveness, for the activity of animals forces us to think in terms, not so much of successiveness, as of conformity to some unchanging pattern.

A third example, and perhaps the most telling, can be taken from psychological science, or everyday experience, whichever you like to call it. Our sense perceptions and thoughts are all characterised by energy exchanges, and therefore exemplify the Second Law of Thermodynamics; but we have something else in us—our *memory*, which works quite differently.

156

Memory escapes from the irreversible character of time. Irreversibility means simply that processes perceived with the senses can never return to their initial state. It is a consequence of the Second Law of Thermodynamics, which is a partial statement of the universal character of time, that all the king's horses and all the king's men cannot put Humpty Dumpty together again. But memory can. Memory can defy the irreversibility of time and take us back into the past. Memory operates by a different mechanism from those upon which depend not only sense perceptions but also the work of the associations, words and signs carried out by the cerebral hemispheres. It is a combinative process rather than a mere repetition. Memory cannot be said to depend on a mechanism resembling a combination of gramophone records. In the characteristic working of memory something goes beyond the mere storing up and repeating of what has gone before.[1] It is the integrative process by which we are sentient beings, and yet it does not operate in time in the same way as our sense perceptions and thoughts. This is not obvious at first sight, but if you want further evidence I would refer you to an interesting discussion of the subject by the late Professor Lloyd Morgan in his Gifford Lectures.

These are but brief descriptions of a very few

[1] At the National Physical Laboratory, a machine is being built which will have a "memory" in the sense of being able to store up and use the results of past operations. Since, however, this makes use of potential energy in the form of electrostatic charge, it falls within the class of the "invisible" process.

examples, but, if you think about it, you will be able to find others in which elements of our own experience somehow stand outside the transience, successiveness and irreversibility of the temporal process.

The next step is to accept the conclusion that *in all reality there are two elements: one which is subject to the conditions of time and another which is not.* It is not hard to see that the element which is subject to the temporal process is the visible part. In the pendulum it is the kinetic energy, the motion, that is visible; in the animal it is activity which is successive and runs down. In our own experience our sensations and thoughts are the temporal activity. The part which cannot be seen is potential energy, the invisible pattern to which the animal conforms, and the place where memory is stored away from time. Reality is not only divided into temporal and non-temporal elements, but these two can be distinguished by the fact that one is visible and the other invisible. The first element conforms to the Second Law of Thermodynamics, the operation of our sense perceptions and the working of our minds. It has all the characteristics of time. The character of the invisible element is different. In everything that presents itself to our experience we find this division between that which is given by our sense perceptions and that which, for various reasons, we infer because what we see around us would not make sense without it. We infer that the energy, which is visible, changes and exists as potential energy at the top of the swing of the pendulum, because dynamics

158

would not make sense without the conservation of energy. We infer that there is an invisible pattern to which the behaviour of animals conforms, because there is no other way in which we can make sense of their activities. We infer that there is something in memory which is more than the working of our sense perceptions, because memory gives us an integration which direct sense experience does not and cannot give. So we have the visible, directly given, and the invisible, which we infer: both equally necessary for a coherent picture of the world.

Having postulated that reality is divided into visible and invisible elements, and agreed that the visible belongs to time, we must now consider the invisible element. Here we are faced with a far more difficult problem. It is perhaps best approached by stating the conclusion, which will be that *the whole of visible reality belongs to time and the whole of the invisible to eternity*. We can then examine the grounds for this conclusion.

We must now go through the familiar process of trying to agree about what we mean by "eternity". This word has been much misused, with the result that nearly all thought on the subject has been confused and uncertain. I shall start by considering a number of senses in which the word "eternity" has been used— just to make it clear that these are not the meanings which I propose to adopt.

Let me state at once that the word "eternity" does not mean an indefinite prolongation of time.

159

J. B. S. Haldane's article, "Time and Eternity",[1] is most disappointing in this respect, for he regards eternity as an infinite prolongation of time, past, present and future. That might, perhaps, be called "everlasting-ness", but more time is still only time; even infinite time is still time. The word "eternity" is wrongly used in any such sense.

Nor should the word "eternity" be used to mean the simple freezing of the present moment. Expressions like "the Eternal Now" are used, implying that in some way or other this moment exists, is crystallised or frozen, and does not disappear. Such a use will not help us with our problem or add anything concrete to our immediate experience; this "frozen now" simply disappears into the past, and does not provide the invisible element in the present for which we are look-ing. Eternity in this sense is a kind of attenuated replica of time which, though by definition free from its perish-ability, remains successive and irreversible and there-fore essentially "time-like".

Philosophers sometimes use the word "eternity" in a way which goes back to the philosophy of the Middle Ages, when men like St. Thomas Aquinas wrestled with the problem of reconciling the impermanence of time with the infinite power and omnipotence of God. They therefore referred to eternity as being the infinite specious present belonging to God, and thought of God as having the whole of time present before Him. This is different from Haldane's use of "eternity" as time

[1] *The Rationalist Annual* for 1946.

infinitely continued; it is time brought together into
some kind of experience belonging only to God, or at
least to beings of a different order from ourselves.
The question whether there is or is not a Being
whose experience is infinitely extended in time is
quite distinct from the question whether there is a
timeless element in all reality, whether experienced
or not.

Finally, there is the use of the word "eternity" to
mean some kind of non-material, non-physical realm,
some world, as it were, of "spirit". In Aldous Huxley's
book, *The Perennial Philosophy*, the chapter on
"Time and Eternity" leads nowhere because he uses
the word "eternity" to express a world of experience
which he regards as non-material and non-physical
and to be entered only by consciousness. This is un
satisfactory because it goes back to the old dualism
between matter and spirit, or matter and mind, which
is the weakest feature of Western philosophy. It implies
the division, made by Descartes, between "thinking
substance" and "extended substance", which led to
what Whitehead called the "Bifurcation of Nature":
two closed worlds, the world of matter and the world of
spirit, between which it is impossible to establish any
sensible working connection, so that according to one's
temperament, as William James declared, one tends
to believe that only the first one is real, or else that only
the second is real. To think about eternity as the
domain of the non-material, entirely separate from our
world of pendulums and animals and men, is no help

L   161 at all in the problem of understanding what it is in the tangible world which in actual fact escapes from the conditions of time.

We must reject these uses of the word "eternity" if we want to find a meaning which will add something significant to our knowledge of the world. To speak of eternity just as a long, or infinite, time is simply bad verbal usage. The idea of a freezing out of the present as an "eternal now" that exists in the present and past, and the notion that eternity is the supernatural, infinite, specious present of God must also be set aside together with the view that leads to the bifurcation of Nature into spiritual and material, mind and matter, or thinking substance and extended substance.

We have now reached a critical stage in our discussion. Having tried as far as possible to clear the ground of all those ways of thinking about eternity which lead only to dead ends, we must try to formulate positively the precise meaning we intend to give to the word "eternity". Let us go back to the division of the world into visible and invisible, and keep in mind also the three characteristics of time: transience, successiveness and irreversibility. What happens if we simply deny these characteristics to eternity and say, when we speak of the pendulum, that in its motion the kinetic energy is transient and must run down and come to a stop, but that its potential energy is not subject to this running down? If we call the latter eternal, we can say that the pendulum swings to and fro in time, but its energy swings from time into eternity and back again. When it swings into eternity it acquires an energy which need not necessarily run down. In the case of a pendulum the potential energy simply returns to kinetic energy, but in the rock on the mountain-top it may remain indefinitely in the potential form. In this potential aspect there is something which does not perish and is not subject to succession. Let us say that this character belongs to eternity.

If we turn from inanimate objects to animals, whatever they may be—whether the paramoccium or the man—we can say that their behaviour always exhibits a running down, a successive passage from birth to death. But what is in eternity is neither transient nor successive. Therefore we can say there is in all animals an eternal pattern that determines their purposive activity, not something which beckons to them from the future or drives them forward from the past, but rather something which is there as part of the animal, just as much as its visible behaviour in time. Although the organism has no *aim* in time, it has an *end* in eternity.

About our human experience let us say that the working of our senses and minds is temporal, but that memory is eternal—or at any rate participates in eternity in a way our sense experience and mental processes do not. Let us go one stage farther with human experience, remembering the different possible levels of human consciousness, and how at different levels of consciousness there can be different degrees of connectedness. Having seen that we are ascribing to

163

eternity the properties of potentiality, structure, freedom of movement, such as we see in memory, as well as independence of the irreversibility of time, we can say that our conscious experience fluctuates between different levels, and that this fluctuation is not a temporal process, but a change of level, or a greater or lesser penetration into eternity. This very idea was suggested by the late Professor McTaggart in *The Nature of Existence*.

Now we can define a little more closely what we mean by eternity. We can say that the characteristics of eternity are that it is free from running down and free from transience; it is the domain of structure and pattern; it is that by which the possibility of choice enters human experience.

This definition of eternity does not connect it with anything remote, belonging to some divine consciousness, or even to a realm of experience apart from matter and things. It is inherent in everything, for everything exists just as much in eternity as it does in time. Eternity is just as much a condition of the existence of a pendulum as it is of the existence of an animal, or of the life and experience of man. We should not regard eternity as something "better" or "higher" than time, as most people who have used the word since the days of Plato tend to do. It is not a realm into which one should endeavour to escape from time. We should rather look upon eternity as the warp upon which the whole pattern of reality is woven. Time is the weft which weaves in and out, but the pattern of life, the pattern of reality, comes from both the permanent unchanging warp of eternity and the incessant recurrence, the incessant return of the shuttle of time through the loom.

Many people have spoken in the past about eternity, and many people speak about it today, but so long as it is relegated to the realm of transcendental knowledge, and so long as pragmatic knowledge is conceived as lying only in time and as referring to processes in time, then those realms must remain separate from one another, and the more pragmatic knowledge advances the less capable does it become of integrating its own discoveries, because there is no warp in the loom. On the other hand, if we think of transcendental values in terms of an eternity which is somehow remote and separate from the things of our experience, we are in danger of becoming artificial and fanciful, because we cannot close our eyes to the immense body of facts which has accumulated in the realm of pragmatic knowledge. That is why the notion of time and eternity, properly conceived, is the bridge which will unite these two realms of knowledge and provide the synthesis for which pragmatic knowledge is expectantly waiting. It will also provide a language in which ultimate values, which are eternal, can be expressed in a way that will be comprehensible for the modern world.

This notion of eternity, although it is so matter of fact and concrete, and must be taken as such, is nevertheless very explosive in its effect upon our thinking about our own problems. You will see this when we develop these ideas further, but we had first to arrive at some degree of common understanding of what I mean by saying that eternity is just as much a condition of all existence as are time and space. *To exist* does not only mean to endure in time and to undergo temporal change. It means also—for everything living or inanimate—to have an underlying pattern from which all its meaning and value are derived. This pattern is not "mere" possibility. It exists and can become conscious. When it does so, there is a fundamental change in the relation of a being to its own destiny. This self-creative process will be the subject-matter of our study in the next few chapters.[1]

[1] Since the lecture on which this chapter is based was delivered, Lowrie's translation of Kierkegaard's *The Concept of Dread* has been published by the Princeton University Press. The discussion of Time and Eternity in Chapter III of that work, concerning the confusion of the future with the possible (pp. 73–82), agrees with that set forth in this chapter.

CHAPTER IX

ESSENCE AND PERSONALITY

WE broke off our inquiry into the psycho-kinetic interpretation of human destiny in order to enlarge our categories of thought and provide ourselves with an additional instrument, the conception of eternity as a determining condition of all reality.

The idea that eternity is a determining condition of every event, in the same concrete way as is time or space, is difficult to grasp, because our knowledge of the external world comes to us through our senses and our minds, which work in time and space. Although this makes us "eternity-blind", we can learn much about the eternal aspect of reality. This knowledge comes by inference from our sense experience: for example, when we infer that in the swinging of a pendulum there is an eternal element, constituted by potential energy, or when we look at living animals and see that there is a norm to which their directive activity conforms, a norm which cannot be explained by reference either to the past or to the future, but can be understood only as something timelessly associated with the organism. These inferences, which derive directly from the careful examination of pragmatic knowledge, are sufficient to justify the conclusion that

167

reality contains, or is contained in, an ampler framework than space and time.

Through our senses we have knowledge of spatio-temporal things. We look at a man's face and see its shape, colour and movements, but we also see other things which we do not perceive in the same way. We may see that he is angry or pleased, that he likes or dislikes us, or we may get a feeling that he is more likely to act in one way than another. This knowledge cannot be explained as inference from our sense perceptions. It is direct knowledge, and it is often present to a high degree in primitive peoples. What we then experience is direct perception of a timeless quality. We have a certain capacity for direct "feeling" or "intuition" of the pattern, as it were, of what is presented to us. Pattern is very important; but clearly there can be different kinds of pattern, and we must come to a common understanding of the word by the same procedure as that we followed in the case of the words "can" and "cannot".

Let us start by thinking of pattern simply in terms of a design, say of a wallpaper or a fabric. This design is a "pattern", which is more than just a collection of coloured patches, because it has a quality of "togetherness" and makes a certain whole, having a significance which the separate parts have not. This is the simplest conception : a design, made by a designer who brings together a number of elements—line, shape, colour, texture—to form a significant whole.

A design or pattern may serve as a model from which

numerous copies are produced. For example, a fabric is designed with a certain pattern, and this pattern goes to the weavers, who make thousands of yards of cloth carrying the same design. There is thus, in the second degree, a certain growth, or potentiality for self-multi-plication, or expansion, inherent in a pattern. This is seen in the work of the dress designer who produces a model dress, from which copies are made all more or less the same as the original. In this there is the further idea of pattern as something with the potentiality of being copied or repeated. This is a one–many relation; from the one model the many copies can be made.

An examination of work that goes with the design of a motor-car will serve to show how potentialities come into being when a pattern is made and how after that there can be the actualisation of those potentialities. The various people concerned in the production of a motor-car write out a specification, agreeing that the new model should be of such and such power, such and such speed, and have certain provisions for the accommodation and comfort of the passengers. Before trying to produce a car to conform to this specification, the Engineering Department will study previous cars and see whether or not existing parts can be improved and brought up to the standard required by the specification. When all this preparatory work has been done designs are made and put together in the form of a prototype, or first model. This is tested, and when everyone is satisfied that, as far as is practicable, the prototype

169

THE CRISIS IN HUMAN AFFAIRS

meets what the specification called for, the manufacturing side will begin to make plans and tools so
that the works can start production. Finally, thousands
or even hundreds of thousands of motor-cars, corresponding to the prototype in all but minor details, will
appear on the road. They are, as it were, the external
visible manifestation of the prototype which remains
hidden away in the Engineering Department.

This is a process by which a certain potentiality for
mass production is created through the work of the
designers. First, there is the development of a potential
as a result of the designers' effort, and then that
potential expands and multiplies into mass production
of enormous magnitude. This is not the whole story,
for if the manufacturers are progressive and far-sighted
they will not long remain satisfied with the model they
have produced. The designers will be requested to go
back and examine the prototype, find out its faults and
prepare a fresh specification. So in course of time an
improved model will appear, and this will have a fresh
potential leading to further processes of production.
The design or prototype has therefore two distinct
destinies, one which is to be actualised in the form of
hundreds of thousands of motor-cars, and the other
which is to be improved and become a new potential
for an improved car. Here we have a third degree of
significance in the conception of moving or advancing
pattern.

The idea of the two-fold destiny of a design is not
confined to the manufacturing process. It can be seen

also in the writing and publication of a book containing some fundamentally new idea, such a book, for instance, as Darwin's *Origin of Species*. For many years the author collects and studies his material, sorts it and uses it for testing his new idea, until at length the first edition of his book is published. Thousands of copies go out into the world, and the ideas expressed meet with mingled acceptance or disapproval in the scientific world. Darwin in the meantime goes back to his farm, studies all the criticisms, and then proceeds to prepare a second—or in his case a third—edition of his book, in which he improves on his first thoughts by all he has learned from the publication of the first edition; and so he accumulates a fresh potential in the form of the new edition of the book. This again is published, and so the process goes on through six or seven editions, building up a potential followed by dissemination in actual form.

There is one further point in these illustrations that is useful to remember. Whereas the process of actualisation is continuous, the change of potential is discontinuous. Between the appearance of one model of the motor-car and the next the design remains stationary. The cars continue to be made substantially, and very often identically, the same as the original prototype. Then, when the new prototype appears, there is a sudden expansion in potential. In the same way, as long as the same edition of the book continues to be printed or reprinted it remains stationary, but when the new edition comes out, a jump forward is made.

These examples make it clear that in the conception of a model or pattern there is a two-fold possibility. On the one hand, the potential for the pattern is actualised in the form of many copies or some other outward result; on the other hand, the pattern itself can develop and change, and become different from what it was originally. This two-fold conception of a pattern can also be applied to the psycho-kinetic and psycho-static doctrines of human destiny.

The psycho-static view is that man has a fixed pattern made once and for all, so that the whole of his life is the more or less successful actualisation of that pattern. He is, as it were, published in a single edition. Whatever potential he has is constant, and what he does is the actualisation of that potential in time. The psycho-kinetic view is that man has a two-fold destiny: he has not only the possibility of actualising his pattern in time, during the course of his life, but also has a different possible destiny, not alternative but super-imposed upon the first, and consisting in the possibility that his pattern itself can change, can grow and become something richer and more significant than it was originally.

This is why the ideas of time and eternity are important. The analogy between man and a mechanical device breaks down at this point, because when we speak of the motor-car we must remember that the actualisation and the building up of its potential in time is not the work of the motor-car itself, but comes from the intelligence of the designer. The fourth degree in the notion of a pattern brings in the idea of the *pattern in eternity*. Man is a being who builds up his own potential, and that cannot happen in time, for that would have to be at the expense of the actualisation of his possibilities. To help us to speak about man from this point of view, I am going to introduce four new terms, which will need a little explanation.

Man has four parts: the first is his *body*. His body is what he himself sees and what an anatomist would find when cutting him up on an operating-table. It comprises the inside and outside of his body, his nervous system, the whole apparatus of the five senses and also the other inner sense that we call thinking.

The next part is the *soul*. By soul I mean nothing more or less than that which distinguishes a living body from a dead body, that element in a living organism which distinguishes it from a thing. It possesses a power which enables it to resist the running down of time, what Schroedinger in his *What is Life ?* calls "the power of the organism to absorb negative entropy from its environment". It is what Claude Bernard referred to when he said, "*La constance du milieu intérieur est la condition de la vie libre*". I do not wish it to imply more or less than that the soul gives living organisms the directive activity about which I spoke, as distinct from the causal mechanisms we can ascribe to non-living matter. This second constituent of man is, like the first, something which he has in common with all living organisms.

The third constituent of man is peculiarly human.

I shall call this *personality*. By personality I mean all that is contained in our experience—all that we have learned from the past, all our views, attitudes, memories, habits of thought and action; all those motives round which our behaviour patterns are constructed. I referred in an earlier chapter to a man as having many personalities, but by "personality" I mean something more than just the sum of these. I mean the whole of what we may call the man's experience from his birth, all he has learned and gained from his contacts with the world.

The fourth part of man is his *essence*. By essence I mean that pattern which is his own unique nature, which is, in him, the potentiality of his existence. The essence of man is what I called in an earlier chapter his "essential nature", which has neither birth nor death.

The way in which these four things stand in relation to the determining conditions of time and space and eternity is shown diagrammatically in Figure 1.

The radiating lines divide the figure into three regions. The region at the bottom comprises both space and time; that on the left, eternity and space; that on the right, time and eternity. The body presents itself to our sense perceptions, it exists in space and time, and you will have no difficulty in understanding what I mean by saying that the body belongs to the space–time aspect of man. The soul is that which keeps the body wound up, as it were, and which prevents it from running down. It cannot therefore have its existence in time, because time is essentially a "passing", or running down, what John Locke aptly called "perpetual perishing". This gives us a sufficient reason for expecting to find the soul, which resists the wearing-out process, in a timeless region. It is therefore placed in the diagram between eternity and space. The soul corresponds to the body in that it has form and

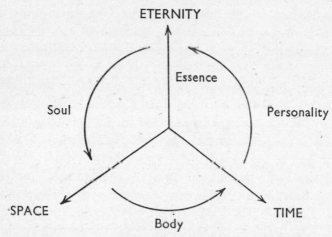

FIG. I. *Man's Four-fold Nature.*

shape, but it also corresponds to the eternal part of man in that it has potentiality or possibility. The soul is therefore the link between the eternal and the spatio-temporal aspects of man, between the essential man and his body.

Personality, on the other hand, is not a bodily thing. It is the sum total of all our habits, attitudes, points of view, motives and so on. These clearly have an element of time in them, but they cannot be put on the line of time because, although they are not held together by something other than themselves, they do not perish with the moment. They have their own power of standing up against time, particularly through memory, the character of which is partly temporal and partly eternal. From one point of view memory runs down, because we forget things; but from another point of view it resists running down, because we can go back and find things again, although the past, or time, has carried them away. Personality is therefore subject to the determining conditions of the region between time and eternity. This will be clearer when I speak of the role of consciousness in relation to personality, and in relation to time and eternity; but for the moment it is sufficient to say that the difference between personality and the body is that the body goes through time by being invisibly wound up, but that the personality stands in a different relation to time : it has something which has foundations in the past and something which reaches out to the future; it has intentions and purposes.

The essence is purely eternal. It is the pure potentiality of man, his pattern taken quite apart from anything which actually happens to it. The essence is "born not, neither does it die; it comes not, neither does it go; unborn, undying, it is not destroyed when the body is slain", as Death says in the "Katha Upanishad".

This diagram shows the importance of introducing the conception of eternity into our thinking, because without it we have no adequate means of speaking about the structure of man. We should have to confine ourselves only to that part of man which we see in space and time, and disregard all that cannot be explained in spatio-temporal terms alone.

These ideas can be developed a little farther by considering the birth of a child, not as any categorical explanation, but simply as an aid to understanding the structure shown in the diagram. The essence of a child is eternal, and therefore is not concerned in birth and death. For birth, three things must come together. The mother and father come together in space and time, but essence is in eternity, without a body, without any physical activity. With conception a body begins to form and take shape. For a time this body depends upon the mother's soul for what I have called its winding up, that is, its ability to sustain existence in time. When it is born, with its first breath it enters upon independent existence in space and time, and at that moment the soul is interposed to link essence and body together. The soul then remains with the body throughout life, to enable the body to renew itself and to conform to and maintain a certain norm of structure and activity. So the mother serves as the instrument whereby a transition from the eternal to the spatio-temporal is possible. The soul itself does not grow or change, but is simply the transmitter of potential to the body. The arrow drawn from left to right in Figure 1 indicates how the potential flows from the essence, through the soul, into the body.

The role of personality is the crux of any inquiry

M

into the psycho-kinetic view of man. It is neither wholly in time nor wholly in eternity, but can at times be more subject to the determining conditions of the one than the other. This fluctuation of personality between time and eternity depends upon consciousness. When the personality is in a state in which the activity pursued is almost entirely time-like—that is, mechanistic and causal—our activity and experience are linked to the automatism of the body. As it shifts in the other direction and orientates towards eternity, the experience associated with the personality becomes more conscious. It can reach a threshold state, in which it has the possibility of exercising the power of choice. The body itself is an automatism, with no possibility of choice, even though it has a soul. When the personality is working on the level of the body, or asleep, it is simply assimilated to the automatism; but as it awakens and comes towards the point at which it is conscious enough to choose, there is present in it a timeless or eternal element which can stand aside from immediate surroundings or events. This we can easily verify for ourselves by examining our own activity and experience. We can easily see that when we have the power of choice we are in a state when there is more than one level of experience present in us at the same time. We are able to stand apart from the automatism of our bodies, apart from the automatism of our minds, and look, as it were, timelessly at this activity; we can choose to say "yes" or "no" to the alternatives that present themselves.

178

We can apply these conceptions to a search for the true meaning of freedom, or free will, and its significance for the psycho-kinetic change which we are trying to understand. With this end in view we must make a distinction between temporal motives and values and eternal motives and values, that is, between pragmatic knowledge and the knowledge of values. In terms of the diagram, pragmatic knowledge is knowledge of what goes on in space and time. Philosophers from Descartes to Kant, from Kant to Bertrand Russell, have taken this to be the only kind of knowledge derived from experience. But knowledge of values is also part of our experience, and this is one of the stumbling-blocks of modern Western philosophy. Knowledge of values—eternal knowledge—is just as direct as that which is given through the senses, but it belongs to a different region. When the personality is awake or in a state of choice it becomes aware of an alternative between activity which partakes more of the eternal and activity which partakes more of the temporal. If the choice is made in relation to the eternal values, the result is to augment the potentialities of the essence, but if it is made in relation to temporal values the result remains in the personality. Thus it can come about that the personality, although it has its activity in time, can contribute something to the life of the essence which is not in time. Thus, as the diagram shows, in the activity of the body as determined by the personality there can be actions of two kinds: there can be actions which are automatisms in which there is no choice, and there can be actions

179

in which there is choice in relation to a system of values outside space and time. If choice is made, something more happens than the mere actualisation of possibilities in time—there is also the building up of a new potentiality in eternity.

No doubt you will be reminded of the saying in the Sermon on the Mount, "Lay not up for yourselves treasures upon earth, where moth and rust doth corrupt and where thieves break through and steal; but lay up for yourselves treasures in heaven, where neither moth nor rust doth corrupt and where thieves do not break through and steal." Of the millions of people who have heard these words and of the many who have been truly influenced by them, there are very few who have understood what is meant by "heaven" and "earth", and because of misunderstandings much difficulty has arisen. So long as we think only in terms of time, if we think at all of another world, we think of the words "future life" and "eternal life" and "heaven" as synonymous. We do not see that the idea of future life and the idea of eternal life are as distinct and as different as they could possibly be. So it comes about that people read passages like this and do not see their connection with other sayings, such as, "the Kingdom of Heaven is within you".

One of the principal difficulties in the formulation of religious doctrines at all times has, in fact, been how to convey to men what is meant by eternal life. If the timeless aspect of eternity is emphasised, people begin to think of an empty annihilation, in the way in which they quite wrongly interpret the Nirvana of Buddhism; or if the avoidance of wrong association is pushed to such an extreme that a mere abstract symbol is used, like the Chinese Tao, people again fail to see its immense significance for our own experience and begin to weave abstract doctrines from it. As against these two, we have the tendency, in the Christian religion, to emphasise the concrete character of eternal life, its real and present character for the individual, and this leads to confused notions of a future life. In this connection there is a strange conflict of expression between the East, where the majority of the religions are based on reincarnation doctrines, and the West, where the majority of religions are based on doctrines of a future life. These two doctrines of the higher destiny of man appear incompatible with one another; but in reality they are both attempts to put into terms which the ordinary unprepared mind can assimilate, a notion which goes beyond temporal expression—the notion that man's real existence is subject to conditions more ample than those of space and time.

In the next chapter I shall deal with the practical interpretation of the diagram, and show how it can come about that a man is able to add something to his essence. The life of the essence does not consist in remaining what it is, but in becoming more. (This idea is given powerful expression in the Parable of the Talents.) For the present I am concerned only to show that when we speak of psycho-kinetic views of man, we should not think in terms of a bare perfectionism, which is a mere conception of self-improvement directed towards the future. The psycho-kinetic conception is something much richer than that, but it is far more difficult to grasp. It is directed not only towards a perfection in the future, but also towards a timeless perfection which neither comes nor goes. As Kierkegaard says:[1] "The synthesis of the eternal and the temporal is not a second synthesis but is the expression for the first synthesis in consequence of which man is a synthesis of soul and body sustained by spirit. No sooner is the spirit posited than the instant is there." This is hard to understand, because our minds are habituated to thinking that everything happens in time. So unaccustomed are we to thinking apart from time, that to speak of a timeless growth of essence is bound for most of us to be using words without meaning; but perhaps in the course of the next three chapters I may be able to help you to catch a glimpse of what they really can mean.

[1] S. Kierkegaard, *The Concept of Dread* (Princeton Univ. Press, 1946), p. 79.

CHAPTER X

THE INFLUENCES UNDER WHICH MAN LIVES

OUR aim is to see whether we can arrive at a positive and convincing interpretation of human destiny. I have tried to show that this is possible only if we are prepared to abandon the exaggerated notion of human importance which has survived both the Copernican revolution and the discoveries of modern astronomy, as well as the repeated failures of human purposes in history. The present crisis in human affairs is closely bound up with the megalanthropic illusion which leads mankind to hope for the impossible. Once an attitude of humility is adopted, the way is open to the acceptance of the psycho-kinetic doctrine according to which the destiny of man is seen in his potentiality for self-creation. This in turn can be rightly understood only if it is related to the conception of eternity as a concrete element in all reality. Once this idea is grasped we are liberated from the false alternatives of pessimism and optimism as to the future.

In this and the next two chapters I shall try to show you how the eternal work of self-creation pervades all time and is invisible only to those who will not look beyond their own "clay-shuttered doors". It would be tedious if I were to repeat at each step the warning that

183

I am not trying to prove what I am saying, but merely showing you a way of thinking about our problems which may lead you to the same conclusions as it has led me. I shall proceed, therefore, on the assumption that you have yourself reached these conclusions and are now concerned to work out their practical implications.

First, however, we must take note of some of the consequences of the psycho-kinetic doctrine in its implication that man is eternal—if we can accept that he possesses, in addition to his temporal life, an eternal life about which neither his senses nor his mind give him any direct knowledge, but which is nevertheless accessible to him in the form of glimpses of a world of immediate values.

If we begin by accepting that our senses are "eternity-blind",[1] how can we establish values that go beyond the temporal, and that cannot be deduced from an intellectual analysis of our sense experience? You will recall what I said about different levels of knowledge, and how we could discriminate conveniently between vegetative knowledge, animal knowledge, pragmatic knowledge and knowledge of values, and that we could regard these as referring particularly to man. Beyond these are higher orders of knowledge which might be

[1] It is very interesting to note that the idea of eternity-blindness was expressed twenty years ago by the great French physicist Louis de Broglie (*Journal de Physique*, 1927, Vol. VIII, p. 67) in a paper called "L'Univers à cinq Dimensions et la Mécanique Ondulatoire". Speaking of the fifth dimension, which is the same as what I have called "eternity", he said, "Les variations de cette cinquième variable échappent complètement à nos sens. . . . Nous sommes comme enfermés dans notre multiplicité espace–temps à 4 dimensions."

possible, but which are certainly not the permanent possession of man such as we know him.

Although man, in so far as he relies only upon the data of sense experience, is "eternity-blind", this does not preclude the exercise of the power of choice, and thereby the increase of his capacity to perceive the eternal aspect of things and reach a level of consciousness in which direct perception of the eternal aspect of reality becomes possible. In other words, we can conceive man as capable of developing an inward vision distinct from the perceptions of the senses, a vision which in his undeveloped state can come to him only in glimpses, leaving him still a prey to doubt and uncertainty as to its validity, but one which, when truly established and confirmed, can lead him on to the possession of transcendental knowledge and the answers to his ultimate questions.

We have thus two levels of mankind: one consisting of those people who have reached such a level of consciousness that they have knowledge differing from ordinary knowledge, and the other consisting of people who have only pragmatic knowledge.

Those who do succeed in reaching the former level realise that what they have experienced is inexpressible in pragmatic language, that is, the language we are accustomed to use in everyday life. This language is based on sense experience, and it is appropriate only for expressing knowledge on that level. Consequently anyone who has acquired transcendental knowledge, in whatever small degree, is faced with the problem, if

185

he wishes to convey it to others, of finding some means of expressing it so that it can be at least partially understood and shared. It is, therefore, very important that we should make up our minds whether or not, and if so, how, the difficulty of language can be overcome. This turns upon the fact that it is possible to communicate experience providing there is a common recognition of the nature of the experience which it is sought to express. This is possible only if there is not too wide a gap between the two levels of experience. We thus arrive at the notion of a chain of communication, each link of which is a small step, but which from one extremity to the other leads from the ordinary pragmatic knowledge of sense perceptions to the transcendental knowledge of eternal experience. It is quite usual for students of this subject to admit that transcendental states of consciousness may be genuine, but in the same breath to assert that they are utterly incommunicable. If this were true they would have no practical importance for the life of those who have not had direct experience of them. We cannot expect there to be only a single link between what is entirely inexpressible, entirely beyond the working of our senses, and the images and mental constructions with which we are familiar in our ordinary lives. In saying all this I want to emphasise that I am speaking entirely about human experience when I use the words "transcendental", "values", "pragmatic". That being so, when I speak about a chain, I mean a chain of transmission by contacts of a kind that human beings can have with one another. This implies a kind of special language and contacts—a structure through which this work of transmitting knowledge can take place.

This idea is a difficult one, and yet it is essential to grasp it in order to follow what I am going to say next. To express it in another way, we can compare a man who is eternity-blind with one who is physically blind, and a man who is able to perceive things under their eternal aspect with one who has normal eyesight. We can at once see in this analogy that the man who is blind is liable to dangers which the man who can see can avoid. There are things which a blind man cannot do which the man who sees is able to do easily; but if the man who can see wishes to help the man who is blind he has to find some means of explaining to him the dangers that beset him, how to avoid them and what are the possibilities his loss of sight still leaves open to him. To do this the man who can see cannot resort to visual images, but must use forms of expression which will have concrete meaning for the blind man. He will have to express his meaning in terms of touch sensations, of what he can hear, and so on. This problem of conveying what cannot be perceived to someone who nevertheless needs to act as though he could perceive it, and in such a way as to enable him to overcome his disability and learn to "see", is at the root of the "doctrine of help" in psycho-kinetic systems.

The doctrine of different levels of being raises the problem of transmitting knowledge from a higher to a lower level. In order to effect this transmission, what I have described as a chain, is necessary. We can now abandon the analogy and use the word "school", by which is meant an organisation for the transmission of knowledge—more precisely, knowledge from one level to a lower level of being.

With this conception in mind, let us return to what I said about the power of choice and the possibility for man of linking the temporal and the eternal in himself. If he chooses in one way he grows in his eternal essence, and if he chooses in another way he merely adds to his temporal process. The question arises, How is he to choose? How can there come to man, whose experience is confined to space and time, any criterion by which he can choose something which, by its nature, is unknowable to him? How can a knowledge of values enter the life of man whose bodily powers, whose senses and whose mind are appropriate only for knowledge which has no quality of values in it? I want to emphasise this point very strongly, because we are so accustomed to taking things for granted that we do not ask ourselves how our sense of value is derived. There is nothing in our sense perceptions which tells us anything about the relative value of things. This is not obvious, but if we think carefully about it we must conclude that there is nothing in the working of our minds which tells us whether or why one thing should be more important than another. If we concede this step, we are forced to draw the momentous conclusion that all human appreciation of value is derived from some other source

than sense perception or reason. For centuries philosophers have disputed the claims of empiricism and
rationalism as the source of valid knowledge; but we
find that we must reject both when it comes to assigning
an origin to our sense of values. Substantially, this is the
conclusion reached by Kant in the Critical Philosophy,
but its practical significance has not been realised by
most people.

This is where the doctrine of levels of being comes to
the rescue. We can say of values in the words of St.
James, "Every good gift and every perfect gift cometh
from above . . .".

The ordinary life of man is lived in a world of sense
perception. His communications with his fellow-men
are by means of language using speech and gesture.
These communications bring him in contact with
various kinds of influences, which can all be grouped
under two heads. I shall call them, for short, influences
"A" and influences "B". The first kind—"A" influences—originate on the pragmatic level. They take
no account of real—that is, eternal—values, but only
of the needs and desires of our bodies and our minds.
In their simplest form they are the systematisation of
animal instincts. In a more complicated way they
include all the characteristically human desires for
success, for power, for security, for comfort and the
good opinion of our fellow-men. These in turn can
lead to a general system of motives which, for all
practical purposes, disregards anything but the visible
and tangible life of man. In other words, influences

"A" are purely temporal in their origin, in the motives they engender and in the actions to which they lead.

Influences of the second kind—"B" influences— always originate in the direct experience of eternal values. They are systematised and transmitted by schools. We can think of such influences in various ways—schools of music, painting, sculpture, literature and the drama—which at one time or another were inspired by the experience of men who had penetrated from the temporal into the eternal. Any schools having such contact or origin will succeed in transmitting a sense of values appropriate to their own form, and will be capable of influencing those who come in contact with them. Or we can think of religious schools. These always discriminate beween temporal and eternal values, and in turn produce influences which directly or indirectly touch man on the pragmatic level. Again, we can think of schools which are concerned with perceptions of values in human relationships—ethical schools—from which codes of jurisprudence or codes of conduct originate, based on the notion that man has responsibilities and duties which do not begin and end with himself. There are also schools of philosophy, which are based on a direct attempt to interpret, in a language which can be understood on the pragmatic level, conceptions which are transcendental in their origin. We can also have schools of another kind, where the very aim and purpose of the school is to establish contact with transcendental experience. These seek to convey their value in a much more direct way than do the other schools I have been speaking about. All these influences belong to what I have called influences of the second kind, or influences "B". They are essentially based on experiences and judgment of value. They always imply, in some way or another, that one thing is more valuable than another—that one thing is more beautiful, or better, or truer, than another, that all that exists can be graded in terms of higher and lower values.

These two kinds of influence act upon man according to his own capacity for discrimination and according to a kind of sensitivity which may be partly in his essence, but is always partly due to points of view which have formed in his personality. But whatever this capacity may be, it enables him to respond selectively to the two kinds of influence. In general, we can say that every man has several personalities, some of which respond more to influences "A", and others which respond more to influences "B". The second kind of influences develop and strengthen motives in him directed to eternal values, and his life will be orientated accordingly. He will begin to form a group of interests that will lead him to seek more of these influences, either from books, works of art, religious teaching or personal contacts. This last item is important, for it will also happen that he will tend to accept relationships with people who are like-minded with himself, and to reject relationships with people who are contrary-minded. He will tend, therefore, to move towards an environment in which the influences of the second kind play a greater part. For this reason, this personality or part of him which gives rise to these interests is given the name "Value Personality". All

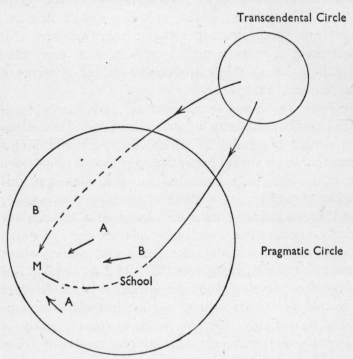

FIG. 2.—*The Pragmatic and Transcendental Circles of Mankind.*

these relationships are shown in diagrammatic form in Figure 2, where our human life is divided into a pragmatic circle and a transcendental circle. In the former are included all people who live entirely by the functioning of their senses, or their intellectual processes. The other is the environment of people who have had direct perception of non-temporal reality. As we cannot have direct connection with the knowledge belonging to the transcendental circle, which is inexpressible in terms of the language which is used in the pragmatic circle, there has to be a chain of schools through which, at each stage, the knowledge is transmitted in forms that become more and more assimilated to the ordinary language until, finally, they appear indistinguishable except for the implications of value which they contain.

At this point we can think of a man, "M", who comes under both kinds of influences, some originating in the pragmatic circle and others in the transcendental circle. The dotted line shows that the latter influences do not reach him directly. According to his response to these influences he will either form, or not form, the value personality. If he acquires this personality it will lead him, instead of remaining in the same kind of environment, to seek one which is nearer to what I have called school ideas. Finally the time will come when he comes into personal contact with a school, and he will then have contact with what I shall call influences of the third kind, or influences "C". The difference between influences "B" and "C" is that the former pass through the ordinary channels of communication, such as the reading of books, enjoyment of works of art and contact with religious teachings. These influences will have passed through many hands and reach him greatly diluted, levelled down or even distorted, so that they may not correspond to the system of values which he really needs. He may not even see that the influences "B" all have their origin in the same kind of experience. All that "B" influences can do, therefore, is to bring about a general discrimination of values, so that greater care will be given to certain things than to others. He will have met the "chain of schools", but he may have met a very weak or attenuated level of school teaching. Should he succeed in coming into contact with a true school of eternal values, he will find himself able to receive knowledge differing from anything he had before, in a much more direct line of transmission, and also—what is of even greater importance—knowledge that is specifically directed towards helping him. Instead of being dependent upon the chance that he may come into contact with something that is useful to him, he will come into contact with people who really know something and who wish to help him in the direction he wants to go. In the simple example of the man who wants to learn a certain form of musical expression, he must come into contact with a school which can give him that particular kind of knowledge.

The general scheme I have outlined is contrary in many respects to much that people assume about the possibilities of changing and development. Many of you may have thought that you were quite prepared to accept the psycho-kinetic view of man, and that you had in fact accepted the idea that we are not completed beings and that we must try to complete ourselves, but

194

you may not have connected this with the idea of "school".

I am now going to make a division between the views of those who think anything of this nature can be achieved by man's own unaided efforts, and those who recognise that, because of our eternity-blindness, we can neither find the starting-point nor even make a beginning relying solely upon our own good intentions. If some sort of start is made, it is not by something we have done, but because there has been working on us some influence of the second kind. Influences of the second kind, however, are not adequate for man to find his own way and to know what it is necessary for him to do and how to do it.

Now, if this is right, it means that great importance is to be attached to the work of schools. I defined schools as organisations for the transmission of knowledge from higher levels to levels at which some degree of knowledge can be assimilated by pragmatic man. This definition can now be expanded by adding that schools are also the means by which pragmatic man can himself ascend the scale and approach the transcendental circle.

Man is not only dependent on schools for knowledge gained on a higher level of consciousness, but he is also dependent on them for help if he wishes to reach that level of consciousness. Quite apart from people who set themselves the task of attaining a higher level of consciousness, there is the question of the whole harmony of human life, which depends upon values being

195

sufficiently well established for people to have common aims and a community of interests without which there cannot be any degree of harmony whatever.

This, really, is what a civilisation means. Civilisations are not held together by ties of blood, but by ties of value. A civilisation embraces a community of all the kinds of value about which I have been speaking, and therefore the very origin and structure of civilisations depends upon the work of schools. So whether we think in terms of individuals or communities, we must realise it is the acceptance of a common system of values that enables communities to live harmoniously and effectively, and we must recognise the work of schools as the foundation upon which all civilisations are built.

This brings me now to a third aspect of the diagnosis of the present world situation, the present condition of human affairs. As I have already said, we must recognise that the epoch in which we live is one in which an exaggerated importance has been attached to man, to his powers and to the place which he occupies in the universe. One result of this is that we place demands and rights before obligations and duties, and coupled with this there is a tendency to regard man as being self-sufficient—that we can find within the human race a complete and satisfactory system of values. This is a fundamental mistake which leads to a growing condition of tension. Another effect of the megalanthropic viewpoint is that false judgments are made in terms of our own good intentions and other people's ineffectual

196

and bad actions. I also spoke about the weakening of values, and how this has caused indifference, apathy and confusion. Over and above these, I will now add that we have to recognise, at this present time, a general weakening in the working of schools as compared with earlier civilisations. Today transmission of value discrimination is less effective than at almost any other period in history known to us.

What I am saying is not new, for people are constantly telling one another that we must return to a sense of values, or that we must return to something or other; but my last word in this connection is that if you have followed what I said earlier about the character of the temporal process, you will see that this conception of a *return*, this trying to restore what has decayed, is essentially false and unrealistic. The problem with which we are faced, the problem that has always faced mankind, is the impossibility of expressing changeless, eternal knowledge in a language which by its nature is constantly in a state of flux and in which the meanings of words are incessantly being modified and distorted. New pragmatic knowledge is introduced, making the old forms useless, and bringing with it new forms of expression. Thus, inevitably, the time must come when the words in which transcendental knowledge was formerly transmitted to men on the pragmatic level cease to correspond to the language which mankind is now accustomed to use. Consequently, it is useless to plead for a return to the old language, which would mean sacrificing new knowledge that has been proved and established on a firm pragmatic basis. The problem is not one of returning to old forms, but of creating new forms by means of which the eternal and unchanging can be expressed, and once more become an effective force in human life. The work of schools is never-ending and never completed; it often lags behind the temporal process to a serious extent, and then, as it were, catches up again. We are passing through a period when the language in which transcendental knowledge was transmitted in the past to people on our level no longer corresponds to the language which we are accustomed to use, and by means of which we can state and verify innumerable facts in our own immediate experience. I shall next attempt to show you how, with the help of the ideas I have so far discussed with you, we can begin to see our way towards a solution of these problems.

CHAPTER XI

SCHOOLS OF VALUE

WE can divide human responsibilities into three categories. First, there is our responsibility towards ourselves—the responsibility of making the best of our own lives. Second, there is our responsibility towards our immediate environment, our family and friends, the people with whom we are in contact and the community or society to which we happen to belong. Third, there are responsibilities which do not arise from our relationships with other people, but come from the feeling that certain things are important, not because of their connection with people, either ourselves or others, but in their own right. Although most people would agree that all our responsibilities fall into one of these three categories, their attitudes towards the whole question will be quite different according to whether they adopt the psycho-static or the psycho-kinetic view of man.

From the psycho-static point of view, responsibility towards ourselves means to make the best of life, to secure what appears to be our own highest welfare. A wise man will see his responsibility towards himself according to the principle, "Whatsoever a man soweth that shall he also reap", but a foolish one will be apt to see it only in terms of his more immediate desires and impulses, without reference to ultimate consequences. In either case, the psycho-static view is that these responsibilities are concerned only with a man's outward experience—with what he does, what he has.

Responsibility towards other people, conceived in psycho-static terms, must refer always to their relation to their environment. If people are themselves taken as unchangeable (except for the relatively trivial case of training which is itself an effect of the environment), then all that can be done for them is to adjust their external circumstances to produce "happiness" or "security" or "freedom", or whatever may be the term used to express an aim that is temporal only. There is clearly a real responsibility of this kind, but it is altogether mistaken to regard it as a sufficient interpretation of human relationships.

Seen strictly from the psycho-static view, there is no reason why the third category of responsibility should exist at all, except as something imposed from without in the form of laws or necessities to which man is subject. He may recognise responsibilities connected with what I have spoken of as values, which enter the life of pragmatic man as influences of the second kind. These influences affect everyone and produce certain points of view and attitudes towards things which are not immediate personal needs or interests; but responsibilities of the third kind appear to anyone who takes the psycho-static view of man, as something imposed from without—in the form of laws, or the will of

200

God conceived as something to which man himself has nothing to contribute.

When the question of responsibility is considered from the psycho-kinetic standpoint quite new factors must be taken into account. A man's responsibility towards himself will be concerned not only with the events of his temporal life, but also with the invisible or eternal part of his existence. He will see that his own personal welfare is bound up with the growth of essence in eternity, so that he will think of his responsibility towards himself in terms of his own inward change. He will see this as something important which is woven together with the affairs of his life in time.

His attitude towards other people will have the same orientation. He will realise that his responsibilities towards them are not only connected with vegetative or animal necessities or with their pragmatic life, but also with their eternal welfare. When he looks at families or larger communities he will judge them, at any rate in part, in terms of the favourable environment they offer for the fulfilment of eternal as well as temporal purposes.

When it comes to the third kind of responsibilities he will see them not as something separate from himself, imposed from without, but as identical with something he has within himself. These three responsibilities will appear as three lines, all converging towards transcendental or eternal values.

This tendency of the three kinds of responsibility to converge when we look at them in terms of the psycho-kinetic view, which takes man as a being able to change and grow in eternity, disappears as soon as we return to the psycho-static point of view. When man's responsibilities are viewed without reference to his own possible change, responsibilities in a community are likely to take the form of utilitarianism, or some way of thinking of the greatest good of the greatest number, which necessarily implies the sacrifice, or partial sacrifice, of the good of some. As soon, therefore, as we begin to see the three kinds of responsibility without reference to eternal values, they fall into three separate and unconnected lines, for there can be no connecting link where everything is taken just as it is, simply as a process going on in time. When human responsibilities are regarded from this standpoint, the world cannot possibly make sense, for it is impossible to harmonise the idea of the welfare of the individual with that of the community without some sacrifice of one to the other.

It is also impossible to harmonise ideas of non-personal responsibilities with the welfare of individuals and communities unless both individuals and communities are seen as moving towards the same values as the larger responsibilities express.

All this may seem very obvious, and it may even appear to you that human responsibilities are in fact rather generally conceived in—what I have called—psycho-kinetic terms. This is where mistakes are very easily made. The general tendency, especially at the present time, is to look towards the future and seek in some better state to be attained *in the future* for the solution of the problems that seem to be insoluble in terms of the present situation alone. There are, broadly speaking, two ways in which people discount the future in order to pay the debts of the present. One is to think in terms of progress towards a better world, and the other is to think of human destiny as a problem which can be solved by accepting some doctrine of life after death, of a world that "rights the disasters of this". It is important to notice that both these ideas imply the realisation that the world of our present experience, alone, as it presents itself to external observation, does not make sense. The attitude towards the present situation, as it stands, is the same whether we think it will make sense when integrated into some future time or some other world outside this. The psycho-static view of man's responsibilities always brings us back to the principle laid down by the White Queen, "Jam to-morrow and jam yesterday—but never jam *to-day*."

Before discussing the question of responsibilities as they appear from the psycho-kinetic standpoint, we must deal with a very usual objection to any suggestion that human motives can be of more than one kind. Some people maintain that no-one does anything except because they want to, or because they think it will make them happier. They insist that all motives spring from self-interest, but that they either can be short-sighted, seeing only the immediate consequences of actions, or can spring from what is called "enlightened self-interest", which looks into the future consequences of actions in a broader way. They say that enlightened self-interest sees how our own welfare must depend upon the welfare of other people, and how man now can find his own welfare in a community where other people suffer, so that all motives return in the long run to the single motive of securing one's own happiness or desires.

This view is based on faulty observation and fallacious thinking. If we look at human behaviour we can find, quite unmistakably, whole groups of actions where the motive is neither short-sighted nor enlightened self-interest, but simply a direct response to the needs of other people. The simplest and most obvious case is the trouble which a mother takes to satisfy the wants of her child. Often there is no pleasure or sense of well-doing in such activity. It is done, as we say, "without a thought". The motive is the welfare of the child, and it is mere sophistry to twist this into enlightened self-interest. There is also a whole group of motives in human behaviour based neither on self-interest nor on interest coming from other people, but in a response to a sense that something outside either of these is valuable or important. There are certain things that people do not destroy, or harm, not from any sense of self-interest, but simply because the question of doing so does not arise, and it would not occur to them that it is *not* worth while putting themselves to a certain amount of trouble to avoid injuring things which are beautiful and valuable.

To discuss this question of self-interest fully would take a long time, and it really does not require any

204

argument at all. I am quite satisfied that anyone who observes carefully can see that motives of the second and third kind are just as real as those of the first, and that what are called self-interested motives are merely bad habits, not coming from any real motive at all. The three kinds are still fairly evenly distributed in human life.

We are not at the moment considering the actions to which these three kinds of motive lead. Each kind of motive can be distorted to such an extent that a man seeking his own welfare will injure himself gravely, destroy his own happiness and bring himself to misery. I tried to show you in the second chapter how motives directed to one's environment may produce results quite contrary to those intended. In fact, all three kinds of motive may produce grave and pernicious results and lead to terrible disasters, but for the present we are concerned only with the stimuli which make people act, and not with the results of their activity.

It may help you to grasp what I have been saying if we try to apply what we have said about motives to the study of history and to the present world situation. A community, whether it is a family or some larger society, may be held together by internal and by external bonds. External bonds may be imposed by some common need, as, for example, the necessity for division of labour or the call for common action to ward off some danger or to attain some common purpose. If, on the other hand, the members of a community have the same or similar conceptions of their welfare as individuals, this will constitute an inner bond between them. If they are interested in one another and feel the welfare of others is important, they will feel a second inner bond. If they have a true community of values, this will constitute a third. When we look at a community such as a family, it is clear that unless there is the inward bond of interest in one another, and desire for one another's welfare, the external bond will merely produce a certain spatial togetherness, an outward community, but inwardly there may be complete division and isolation of the members one from another.

This inward bond in communities, this interest of members of the same community in the welfare of one another, spreads outwards. If we think of an individual we can see how it extends first towards his own immediate family and then to his friends. The strong feeling of desire for the welfare of one's immediate circle spreads quite a long way through the society or groups to which an individual belongs, but as it spreads and touches larger and larger numbers of individuals, its unifying power grows less and less, until finally it reaches the point at which no feeling of unity is engendered. Then a new kind of relationship, implicit in such words as "strange" and "foreign", begins to enter.

A convenient name for the group which is the utmost limit to which this unifying influence can go, is "the nation". No precise "real" meaning is to be attached to the word " nation ". It represents a way of grouping families in terms of a centripetal influence of kinship. "Nation" in this sense does not necessarily refer to any particular kind of geographical boundary, and certainly does not imply any racial or political doctrine: it simply covers the particular group within which an individual can have, towards another, the feeling of "fellow-countryman", and beyond which he has the feeling of "stranger" or "foreigner". The limitations of this group are different for different people. Some feel that people living in the next county are strangers or foreigners, and others have a sense of union over a much greater area. This sense of unity in a group is felt differently at different times and with differing means of communication; but throughout recorded history there have always been natural groupings that can be looked upon as nations.

We must clearly distinguish between a nation and a state. The latter is a pragmatic organisation rendered necessary by the forces which make for misunderstanding and conflict. A state may or may not have the same boundaries as a nation. The belief that a state can "do" is a typical megalanthropic fallacy.

The boundary of the nation is the limit beyond which the second kind of motive will not stretch, but if we look at the third kind of motive we can readily see that so long as there is a community of values, a positive relationship remains even where there is diversity of language, race, climatic conditions, habits, customs and environment—all in fact that goes to make a nation.

In literature and art, there can be community of values in the recognition of what is beautiful and

207

valuable. There can be community of values in the sense of right and justice, which springs from a common understanding of law and order. Above all, there can be a real community of worship and religious values. Such a community of value, taken together, constitutes the third kind of bond, produced by motives of the third kind. It provides a link which can unify much larger numbers of individuals than motives of the second kind. The whole grouping within which this community of values exists may conveniently be called a civilisation, using the word very approximately in the same sense as in Professor Toynbee's *A Study of History*, and classing as civilisations all groupings and peoples such as those we call "Western civilisation", or the "Graeco-Roman civilisation", or the "Chinese civilisation". A number of such civilisations, with fairly well defined frontiers and no great degree of inter-penetration, may flourish simultaneously in different parts of the world.

Where there is a community of values or a civilisation, a corresponding personal bond will exist between individuals so that it will be impossible for conflicts and tensions to increase beyond a certain degree. Within a civilisation the worst and most cruel kinds of wars and conflicts, such as arise when races confront one another feeling that they have nothing in common, can never arise. One aspect of this is seen in the cruelties perpetrated in religious wars where the community of values has broken down.

The community of values on which civilisations

208

depend does not flow outward from the individual, but inward from the values themselves. We have already seen how doctrines and conceptions of values do not arise spontaneously from the ordinary operation of our pragmatic experience. This comes from our sense

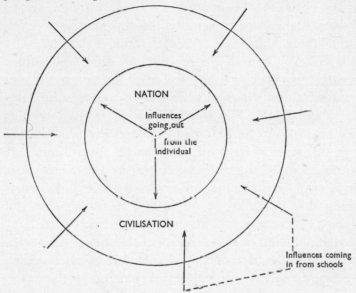

NATION

Influences going out from the individual

CIVILISATION

Influences coming in from schools

FIG. 3.—*Nations and Civilisations.*

impressions and from thinking about our sense impressions. Values come from higher levels of experience and are transmitted through various channels to the ordinary pragmatic level. An individual has personal relationships stretching at their utmost limit to the nation, which may form part of a larger grouping or civilisation. The essential difference between nations and civilisations is illustrated by the diagram, Figure 3.

o

A civilisation grows up as a result of a different process from that which brings a nation into existence. A nation comes into existence by the natural extension of the family to the clan, and from the clan to the group of clans that intermarry freely. A civilisation arises through the appearance of a common set of values. Values are transmitted to the pragmatic level, from their source in transcendental experience, by schools. We can therefore conclude that civilisations are the work of schools, and that the community of values and traditions on which they are based originates in school work. The word "schools" is used here in the same sense as before, to denote any organisation for the transmission of knowledge from higher to lower levels. It must also be emphasised that the values with which schools endow civilisations include everything that is felt to be important, in the sense of St. James's "every good gift and every perfect gift . . ." as distinct from ordinary personal experience connected with the vegetative or animal concerns of men or their affairs at the pragmatic level. According to this interpretation of the diagram, it appears that when the work of schools is active, whether they are schools of art, philosophy, jurisprudence or religion, civilisations will grow and gain strength; but when such work weakens or diminishes, the values upon which civilisations are built tend to become assimilated into the ordinary pragmatic levels of experience, and the unifying influence, on which their very existence depends, will cease to be effective.

I should distinguish one further stage beyond what I have been defining as a civilisation. This is what—in the first two chapters—I called an Epoch. An epoch is characterised by a grand conception, a Master Idea, which inseminates the whole life of mankind for a new harvest of temporal activities. The Master Idea of our present epoch is the *value of the human individual*. Originally this idea was entirely psycho-kinetic in its call to mankind. It has so degenerated that it has become the core of psycho-static creeds, which deny or disregard eternal values. It is easy to see that the Master Idea of an epoch plays an entirely different part in history from that of the value system of a civilisation. Both come from schools, but schools of different levels.

We are today at the end of an epoch, and the Master Idea of the new epoch has not yet emerged. In the meantime men seek to repair the decayed civilisations of the world. They do so in outworn meaningless terms—Freedom, Communism, the Individual, the State. All these are derivatives of old systems. A typical example of a meaningless, pseudo-value system can be seen in the so-called Atlantic Charter. Its values, which are taken as self-evident—even platitudinous—are the psycho-static motives which derive from the vegetative and animal level of man, and certain ideas connected with his pragmatic experience. They scarcely refer at all to the eternal values which are the sole true source of unity in a civilisation. We have before us in this document the exact symptoms of the way in which such remnants of value ideas as exist are tending to be assimilated into the pragmatic level. At such times as these there is always a strong tendency to relapse into the kind of unity which belongs only to a nation.

Let us now return and consider the three kinds of motive viewed from the psycho-kinetic standpoint. If we think in terms of the motive which drives a man to seek his own welfare, we realise at once that he needs not only to desire his own welfare, but also to know how to secure it. As soon as he begins to realise that his welfare is not to be found on the pragmatic level, he will begin to acquire a "value personality", and will feel the need of contact with school work and with an organisation which can transmit to him at least some element of true values.

His attitude towards other people will be determined by the realisation that what he can give to them, and what he can take from them, depend very much upon whether both he and they understand the nature of their true welfare. He will see also that neither he nor they can realise their true welfare unaided, but that they both need to be in contact with some form of organised work in which the limitations of pragmatic knowledge can be overcome.

He will see that the aims and purposes people set before themselves must necessarily be ephemeral and subject to the disintegrating influence of time, unless they have some eternal element or pattern to which they are seeking to conform. All the three kinds of motive therefore converge for him, and he will come to see, more and more, that the three are in reality one and that in seeking his own welfare he must also seek the welfare of others, but he can contribute nothing towards the welfare of other people unless he himself changes and acquires knowledge and powers through which he can help them. He will also see that he can contribute nothing towards the realisation of any eternal aim, or the fulfilment of any eternal purpose which is invisible on the pragmatic level, unless he can wake up and see it for himself.

Looked at from the psycho-static point of view, life seems incoherent, devoid of any integrating principle, but from the psycho-kinetic point of view it begins at once to make sense; the very difficulties with which people have to struggle are seen not as something to be overcome in the future, or to be compensated in another world, but as immediate necessities for securing the welfare which they seek both for themselves and for other people, and for the work which they feel to be important above and beyond themselves.

It must be understood that these three kinds of motive pervade the whole of human life. It is also necessary to understand that if these motives operate in the absence of value knowledge, in the absence of discrimination between real and illusory, or between eternal and temporal things, they can produce disastrous results. We can also realise that these motives are a driving force in human life, but we must at the same time remember that they are not sufficient by themselves; they need knowledge of methods before they can be endowed with psycho-kinetic power.

213

We are passing through a transitional stage in human history, when it is necessary that there should be a return to the active creation of values upon which all effective community of interests depends, and without which there cannot be anything but conflict and disaster. I have tried to show you some of the causes of this state of affairs, and our last task will be to draw from our studies such conclusions as we can about the needs of our present position and the problem of the future.

CHAPTER XII

THE ETERNAL ROLE OF SCHOOLS

OUR aim in these studies has been not merely to sound the knell of a dying epoch, but to seek for a positive understanding of the human problem. We cannot be satisfied with the recognition of failure of a particular purpose, but must look for a line of action which will be free from the destructive elements which pervade so much of human life. It is characteristic of the present time that it is assumed as axiomatic that purposive, intentional activity must aim at fulfilment in future time. I have tried, above all, to convince you that this assumption is unwarranted. Time, as I have tried to convey its nature to you, is the realm of means. Ends and their fulfilment belong to eternity. This conception is as ancient as mankind, but it is always new and astonishing to those who have been accustomed to believe that to exist can only mean to exist "in time". We must, therefore, once again seek its implications for the particular question we are trying to answer —the question of *what to do in the present state of world affairs*.

If we accept it as an axiom that all fulfilment must belong to the future, we are inevitably led into some kind of evolutionism, according to which not only animals and man, but values and institutions, evolve, and, what is more important, even that which is higher than man, even God, evolves. The doctrine that everything is passing from a bad past through a fairly good present to a better future is quite widely accepted, though perhaps not in such crude terms. In this country it is associated particularly with the name of the philosopher, Professor S. Alexander, who specifically speaks of God as evolving and regards the whole universe, including its Creator, as incomplete and moving towards some greater perfection in the future. This doctrine is the essence of Alexander's book *Space, Time, and Deity*, but although he brought the notion of universal evolution to its logical and inevitable conclusion, the same idea is inherent in other evolutionary teachings, such as those of Bergson and Lloyd Morgan.

Alexander is also responsible for the famous saying that we should "Take time seriously". This is quoted with approval in many present-day philosophical writings, and almost invariably interpreted as meaning that we should see our values in time future.

Whitehead has pointed out that the writings of philosophers like Alexander and Bergson do not deal with the very serious contradiction between their view of the world and the fact that our experience does not conform to the universal betterment which they postulate.

The Second Law of Thermodynamics, which Eddington has called the best-established and possibly the most certain of all the laws of nature, is no novel idea or recent discovery of research, but corresponds

216

to our own universal and invariable experience that everything wears out and grows old. At all times writers, poets, artists, and all those who interpret the world by their feelings, have striven to express their sense of the running down which is inherent in the temporal process; the same conclusion, formulated in other words, is reached by mathematicians and physical scientists who come to it by thinking and by methods of exact measurement. Philosophers who accept an evolutionary view, however, ignore this law altogether—as, for example, Alexander does in *Space, Time, and Deity*, in which there is scarcely a reference to the problem it presents. The same is true of Bergson's writings, and of Lloyd Morgan's *Emergent Evolution*. Philosophers who do not ignore the Second Law of Thermodynamics but accept its full implications arrive, like Bertrand Russell, at a doctrine of stark pessimism about our own condition and the condition of the world in which we live. As people look at the world today, there is no third way out of the dilemma of hope and despair. We recognise that the world in which we live does not make sense. We think that, unless we can look forward to its making sense—or at any rate more sense than it now does—in the future, the position is hopeless.

This dilemma comes from the failure to *take eternity seriously*, the failure to recognise that eternal values are exempt from the temporal process. Adapting the words of the Upanishad, we may say that Value is born not, neither does it die, it comes not, neither does it go, unborn, eternal, firm and everlasting; Value is not subject to the Law of Death. If we take the view that values do not evolve, but are eternal, and not subject to the temporal process, we find the sanction and meaning of life not in future time, but in the weaving together of eternal purposes and temporal endeavours to create a pattern which has no beginning and no end; but which nevertheless gives to every moment of time a rich significance which no purely temporal activity could ever possess.

The question which confronts us is whether we are entitled to think in this way, or whether it is just a different kind of unjustified optimism to do so. To answer this it is necessary to understand what is meant by timeless values in general and more particularly to understand the nature of "purpose without because". One or two examples may help to make the meaning clear, even if they cannot be entirely convincing.

In our own personal private experience each one of us can search our memories and find the moments in our lives which we consider most important and most precious to us, and then decide whether their significance was derived from some relation to a future. It does not matter whether we have had experience of higher states of consciousness, or whether we merely think in terms of the brightest and most precious of ordinary experiences, almost every one of us will agree that such moments and experiences, if we look at them carefully, bear their own values, and do not gain significance from any "because". From such researches it is possible to catch a glimpse of the meaning of eternal values and to realise that it is not necessary always to look to the future to find purpose and meaning in the events of life.

We can see this same timeless element in the work of the artist who strives to express some vision of beauty. His perception is essentially timeless ; does not belong to the past or the future, or even the present. It is, as it were, a glimpse of a pattern in a moment which does not come or go. This experience is timeless, and therefore ineffable. The artist is the instrument by which it is translated from eternity into time. In this work there is no "because", for the vision is the active force, and it takes hold of him so that the direction of expression is from the pattern to the realisation rather than from the artist's intention to achieve some form of expression in the future. He may think, and possibly act and even interpret his actions, in ordinary terms, of purposes to be attained in the future; but if the work has any true value there will always be a part from which "because" has disappeared. I do not, of course, mean to suggest that the artist is always "possessed" by his work in this way, or that he is free from temporal motives. I want only to remind you that this experience of feeling oneself the instrument of a vision that has no "because", is by no means rare and is attested by many of the world's greatest artists. Balzac, writing about the work of the novelist, describes how the world of his people took charge and how his own intentions disappeared. It is probable that all writers have at some time found the same thing happening to

219

them. One or two letters of Mozart refer to the process of composition in his own work in a most illuminating way. He once described how the whole pattern of the work appeared to him almost inverted in its order in time; he said it all happened as though he began from the end and afterwards found himself at the beginning. These accounts are very interesting, because the writers are groping after a description, in ordinary language, of the relationship between the eternal pattern of values and its temporal expression.

The examples of purposive action not related to future aims which can be found in religious experience are the most important and decisive of all. It is quite evident that what is called mystical experience never finds its sanction in terms of results in the future. Whatever else we may think or understand about it, we have to recognise that all experience of this kind has the same common element. If mystical experience were—as is often supposed—something rare which comes only to a few people of unusual type, we should not be justified in drawing important conclusions from their descriptions. If, however, we study the subject attentively, we can see that it is a matter of degree. The great mystics, like the great artists, have the vision of timeless reality in a far higher degree than the majority. But most of us have had glimpses which should make us confident that the distant peaks are made of the same solid rock as the lower heights upon which we ourselves have stood. I call them "solid rock" because they convey a feeling of reliability and unfading

220

strength which is quite absent from our ordinary experience of the temporal flux.

If mystical experience is perhaps too private to be taken as concrete evidence of timeless reality, we can turn and examine the foundations on which all the great religions have been built. In the origins of all these religions we find conceptions in which time and the future play no part. The Chinese founders of Taoism always emphasised that the "perfect Man" acts without "because". We see this in the reiterated phrase of Chuang Tzǔ about "flexibly, following the course of nature" no less than in the positive denial of future purpose in the Tao Tê Ching. The Hindu religion, in the teaching given in the "Bhagavad Gita" and the great Upanishads, laid great stress on action without reference to the fruits of action, on the vanity of purposes and desires, and denied emphatically that the reason for action should ever be sought in the aim of obtaining results in the future. In the Christian teaching of the Gospels the same thing is explicitly stated in such words[1] as, "Take no thought for the morrow", and implied in the central prayer, which is the basis of all prayer, "Thy Will be done". The Prophet of Islam insisted in no less degree on the necessity for giving up human intentions towards some future project in time, and the entire acceptance of God's will.

This insistence that the sanction for action is not in

[1] Strangely at variance with the avowed eschatology of the teaching of Jesus.

some purpose to be achieved, is the one element which is completely common to all the great religions in their earliest forms, the nearest to the time of their revelation. It has been rightly said that the worst compromise which the Christian Churches have made, out of all the terrible compromises of the last 2,000 years, was to accept evolutionary ideas, which put values into the future. Although this compromise undermines completely any religious conception, we must recognise that the whole world has tended in recent centuries, and particularly at the present time, to think in terms of purposes which envisage some future fulfilment. This attitude has either carried away or blunted men's sense of eternal values. It has made them blind to the beauty of actions without "because".

This rather long introduction to the notion of actions without "because" was necessary in order to sum up the principal theme of these chapters. This is the importance of trying to restore the true balance between time and eternity in our understanding both of our own motives and of the meaning of life.

The problem with which we are faced can be stated very simply. The psycho-kinetic doctrine asserts that man can change his essential nature. But the very word "change" seems to imply change *in time*. What then is the meaning of "actions without because"? In other words, how can we reconcile the idea of an eternal goal with that of a temporal path? If we cast our minds back to the diagram on page 175, which shows the relation between the spatial, temporal and eternal parts

222

of man, or between body, soul, essence and personality, it is clear that the growth of man does not depend so much on change towards the future as on the enrichment of his essence. We saw how this enrichment came from exercising the power of choice, which the personality does in the light of what it has learnt and understood about values. This relation between the personality and essence requires that when we begin to take eternity seriously, we must not cease to take time seriously. Taking eternity seriously must not be mistaken for a form of quietism according to which the only aim worth striving for is escape from time altogether. On the contrary, we must look upon life as a tapestry in which time and eternity are woven together, and in which time serves for work and eternity for fulfilment. There can be no sense, but only contradiction, if we think of time as the place of both work and the fulfilment of work, because the very nature of time is that nothing in it can ever be finished or made permanent. Eternity is the realm of ends, and time is the realm of means; fulfilment is in eternity, but time is the workshop. Once this idea is grasped it becomes clear that the psycho-kinetic doctrine is in no way opposed to, but confirms, the view that one must not look for fulfilment of purposes in time.

The saying from the Sermon on the Mount, "Take no thought for the morrow . . . sufficient unto the day is the evil thereof", must therefore be taken quite literally; but these are very difficult words, and much

223

thought is needed for their understanding. Every process has its own time, its own day. The day for us is not the whole twenty-four hours, the day for us is that brief moment in which the power of choice is present in us. It is of this moment that we must take thought, and we must exercise the power of choice at the moment when it comes to us, because if we think beyond this moment, of what we shall do even one moment later, we lose its possibilities.

So for us this injunction has an even stranger meaning than at first sight appears. We must take no thought, not only for the morrow, but even for the very next moment. It is for this present moment that we must take thought. In our sleeping state our whole power of choice is in the moment. A man who has woken up and who can speak of "day" and mean a whole day certainly has to take thought for something bigger than one moment. Schools, if we think of them as organisations which are awake and working on a higher level of consciousness than ours, may have an even longer day, which may embrace greater regions of space and time; but the essential thing is to understand —whether we are taking thought for the immediate moment (that is, the day for us, such as we are) or whether we are thinking of the longer days which can belong to conscious organisations and structures—that there is always the absence of "because", the realisation that the work, whatever it may be, is its own justification. If I say at this moment, I must choose to be awake, I make the choice because to be awake is a better state than sleep, not because it will produce some beneficial results tomorrow.

Now let us try to bring together all the threads of what we have been discussing in these twelve chapters. First, we must think again about the present situation of the world, and of mankind, and see how we can interpret it in the light of what we have been saying. We must recognise that the balance between time and eternity has scarcely ever in recorded history been so gravely disturbed as it is at the present time, and that the emphasis has been thrown entirely on time to the virtual neglect and disappearance of eternal values.

We have also spoken about knowledge and being. Man's being is what he is and how he stands in relation to his own inward powers, and his knowledge on this level is largely what we called "pragmatic" knowledge. Here again there is an extraordinary disappearance of natural harmony in the world. Mankind has grown worried, anxious, irritable, unable to use and unable to master the knowledge which it has acquired. This state of anxiety has become more marked during the last two centuries.

The same thing can be put in another way if we observe the disequilibrium which exists between rights and duties. In the world today individuals, families, communities, nations and civilisations, everywhere, insist upon their rights and lack a corresponding recognition of their duties and responsibilities. We must recognise that this disequilibrium cannot be set

P   225 to rights on the pragmatic level, for it is precisely over-emphasis of all that belongs to the pragmatic level that has caused the disequilibrium.

Dangers and tensions become far more acute when large masses of the world's population confront one another than they do at times when communities are smaller, but the present situation springs from something deeper and more serious than this, for underlying all the lack of balance is a background of the arrogance and self-importance of man, the attitude which I called megalanthropism. The epoch in which we live achieved its greatness through the Master Idea of the significance of man as an individual. The psycho-kinetic doctrine has revealed the truth of this Idea. The psycho-static view which now dominates the world is its degeneration. The parable of the Gadarene swine is repugnant to those who think in megalanthropic terms. But to the eye which sees *sub specie aeternitatis* it is a true picture of man possessed by the devil of isolated self-importance. The fate of the infatuated herd is clearly before us all. Well-intentioned people believe that we can remedy this terrible situation by various kinds of political and social constructions and reconstructions, but all these schemes belong to the pragmatic level and are based on the assumption that man can *do*, that his actions can correspond to his intentions.

If we look back over the past few centuries, we can see how much these well-intentioned endeavours to create better material conditions on the pragmatic level, at the inevitable expense of eternal values, have

226

contributed to the present accelerated decline in human affairs. We can see how the whole of human society has brought itself under the laws of time which are the laws of degradation and degeneration, and there is no power left which can free them from these laws. We must recognise that the catastrophe cannot be averted, and that the pretences which we continue to cherish will have to break down completely before anything can be rebuilt. No possible kind of reconstruction or rearrangement on the pragmatic level can arrest the process of dissolution.

A catastrophe is inevitable, but we do not know when it will come. We are speaking now of events on a scale not measured in years but in generations. The megalanthropic epoch started a hundred generations ago, in the fifth or sixth century B.C., with the emergence of the Grand Idea and a general revolution of thought all over the world. It produced new and improved conditions of life by enabling many experiments and innovations to be made in the life of man, but it carried in itself the seeds of its own dissolution in the exaggerated importance which it attached to mankind. That whole epoch is now coming to an end, but no one can measure within one or two generations when the process will culminate in the final catastrophe.

We must therefore look around us and see whether we can perceive any signs of hope that out of this unavoidable ruin something may emerge which will create possibilities for building up something which will not necessarily be better, for that is

227

not important, but which will be eternal and therefore new.

There are various trends to which we can point. Some are psychological, such as the presence in the world of many people who have formed in themselves value personalities, with an attraction towards eternal realities. We can also see how, at times when the external conditions of life are most terrible—as has occurred in our own times, in countries which were invaded and cities which were bombed—a new kind of relationship between man and man appeared, if only for a short time. That kind of relationship was, and is bound to be, a source of the greatest encouragement to anyone who has experienced it, because it teaches us that when man is brought sufficiently low and has been shorn of arrogance, what is left is not something worse, but something better. Then again the advances of ordinary pragmatic knowledge are beginning to supply a corrective for the exaggerated importance which we have been in the habit of attributing to all that concerns the human race. The advance of astronomy makes it impossible for us to think any longer that this planet is supremely important in the universe, and this realisation induces a new humility about the significance of man in the scheme of things. The progress of biological science, as well as better understanding of physiology, has shown how many of the things which we used to ascribe to moral character should really be regarded as the result of physical conditions. These new developments force us to revise our views on the degree of responsibility which we can attach to the actions of the human individual. We look outside to the stars or inside to our nervous system and endocrine balance, and cannot but see that we need to be much more humble about man and the degree of importance and responsibility he has in the world.

At the moment, these realisations are completely masked by the force of the megalanthropic tradition and by the credit which we take for our ability to blow things up and scuttle about at hundreds of miles an hour; but as we begin to be a little less proud of these achievements the progress of science will begin to prepare our minds for a different and very much more humble attitude towards man.

So we may expect that if certain conditions are fulfilled a new period or a new epoch may begin, and the balance between time and eternity will be restored, so that it may be perceived that the greater part of human suffering comes from our present evil tendency to look towards the future for what is important.

The first condition that must be fulfilled before this can come about is that knowledge and guidance should come to us from a higher level. It is the very essence of all we have been saying that we should realise that on any given level the possibility of rising to a higher level depends upon help. If we think in terms of eternal values, we must realise that these are not to be found, like pennies in the street, by people who know only how to walk on the ground, they have to be brought to us through the intermediary of those who have had true experience of what we have called transcendental knowledge. We have seen that the values are the bond of civilisation, and that civilisations have their origins in the work of schools. It is above all at times like these—the winter-time when seeds are sown—that the work of schools is necessary. We may not see the time of harvest, but we know, if we look at everything that the past can teach us, that the seeds have always been sown when the ground has been ripe. We cannot tell how or when this seed-time will come. We have not yet even heard "The voice of one crying in the wilderness and saying, Prepare ye the way of the Lord". But any understanding we may have gained about time and eternity, either from the study of the past or by interrogating our own experience, must convince us that the work that reaches down from higher levels to lower levels is always there. The difficulty is now as it was when these same things were spoken of 2,000 years ago, that "this people's heart is waxed gross and their ears are dull of hearing, and their eyes they have closed, lest at any time they should see with their eyes and understand with their hearts and be converted".

I have referred many times to the fact that we are all asleep, but all that I have said must make it clear that our responsibility towards ourselves, towards other people, and towards those things which are beyond our personal concern, is that we should seek a way to ensure that our ears shall not be closed and that our eyes shall

230

THE ETERNAL ROLE OF SCHOOLS

be able to see when the time comes. This is the aim of
the psycho-kinetic attitude to man, the opening of
possibilities in our essence, the opening of the inward
eye and of the inward ear, which are able to perceive
indications coming from a different level. If we have
seen the character of the situation which confronts the
world, and if we look ahead over the next period, we
see that we entirely depend upon help of a very different
kind from any that we can see around us today. The
essential difference between an Epoch and Civilisations is that the former originates in Revelation from
beyond humanity, while the latter are the work of
schools within humanity itself. If I am right in the
conclusion that we are witnessing the end of an Epoch
and not the transition from one form of civilisation to
another, we must place the hope of the world in a fresh
Revelation of the Divine Purpose to Mankind and
prepare ourselves to be ready to receive it.

INDEX

232

Emergent Evolution (Lloyd Morgan), 217
Ends belong to eternity, 215
Endocrine system, 122
Energy, kinetic, 154
Energy, potential, 154
Epoch, 24, 211, 231
Epoch, end of an, 113, 227
Epoch, hemitheandric, 22
Epoch, Master Idea of, 211, 226
Epoch, megalanthropic, 23, 32, 125, 227
Epoch, new, the coming of, 129
Epoch, new, seeds of, 127, 230
Eschatology, 221
Essay on the Human Understanding (J. Locke), 74
Essence, 66, 174, 188
Essence and personality, 167, 223
Essence, as eternal pattern of man, 168
Essence, growth of, 201
Essence purely eternal, 176
Essence, timeless growth of, 182
Essential nature of man, 133, 135, 137, 139, 142, 174
Eternal life, 180, 184
Eternal Now, 160
Eternal pattern, 163
Eternal role of schools, 215
Eternal values, 229
Eternal value system, 125
Eternity, xiv, 145, 148, 175
Eternity and thermodynamics, 162
Eternity as eternal pattern of man, 168
Eternity as invisible element of reality, 159
Eternity as realm of self-creation, 172

Eternity as universal condition of existence, 161
Eternity-blind, man is, 167, 184, 187
Eternity-blindness, 195
Eternity, definition of, 159
Eternity not non-material spiritual realm, 161
Eternity to be taken seriously, 217, 223
Events, control of, 30
Everlastingness not Eternity, 160
Evolution doctrines not be identified with psycho-kinetic dd., 134
Evolution, theory of, 29
Exaggeration of human power, 90
"Except a man be born again", 141
Existence as "more" or "less", 55
Expectations usually falsified, 101
Experience, as three-storied house, 20
Experience, communication of, 186
Experience, solid rock of, 220
Experiment and inference, 110
Experiment, knowledge derived from, 28
Experiment on being awake, 76, 77
Expression of values temporal, 118
External world, knowledge of the, 153

Fact, knowledge of, changes with time, 118
Fact, problems of, 111

234

235